gods of rock

Rob Fitzpatrick
and
Mark Roland

Main Street
A division of Sterling Publishing Co., Inc.
New York

10 9 8 7 6 5 4 3 2 1

Library of Congress Cataloging-in-Publication Data Available

Published by Main Street, a division of Sterling Publishing Co., Inc.
387 Park Avenue South, New York, NY 10016

First Published in Great Britain in 2005 by
Think Publishing
The Pall Mall Deposit
124-128 Barlby Road, London W10 6BL
www.think-books.com

Text © Think Publishing and GCAP Media plc 2005
Design and layout © Think Publishing and GCAP Media plc 2005
The moral rights of the author have been asserted.

Written by Rob Fitzpatrick and Mark Roland
Edited by Emma Jones
The *Gods of Rock* team: Christopher Bennett, James Collins, Rica Dearman,
Rhiannon Guy, Matt Packer, Mark Searle, Lou Millward Tait and Suzi Williams

Distributed in Canada by Sterling Publishing
c/o Canadian Manda Group, 165 Dufferin Street
Toronto, Ontario, Canada M6K 3H6

For information about custom editions, special sales, premium and
corporate purchases, please contact Sterling Special Sales
Department at 800-805-5489 or specialsales@sterlingpub.com.

ISBN-13: 978-1-4027-3673-5
ISBN-10: 1-4027-3673-8

Printed & bound in Singapore by KHL Printing Co.
The publishers and authors have made every effort to ensure the accuracy and currency of
the information in *Gods of Rock*. Similarly, every effort has been made to contact copyright
holders. We apologize for any unintentional errors or omissions. The publisher and authors
disclaim any liability, loss, injury or damage incurred as a consequence, directly or
indirectly, of the use and application of the contents of this book.
Cover image: Bettmann/CORBIS

**I don't listen to music.
I hate all music.**

Johnny Rotten

THE AUTHORS WOULD LIKE TO THANK:

Mark for being the best co-writer a man can have, but especially to Silvana and Fabio for going swimming above and beyond the call of duty.

CONTENTS

Top of the pops

RECORD MAKERS, BREAKERS, AND FAKERS

ROLLING STONE'S 20 GREATEST ALBUMS

In 2003, *Rolling Stone* magazine published a Special Collector's Issue of what they considered the 500 greatest albums of all time. Here are the top 20 from that list:

1. *Sgt. Pepper's Lonely Hearts Club Band* – The Beatles

2. *Pet Sounds* – The Beach Boys

3. *Revolver* – The Beatles

4. *Highway 61 Revisited* – Bob Dylan

5. *Rubber Soul* – The Beatles

6. *What's Going On* – Marvin Gaye

7. *Exile on Main Street* – The Rolling Stones

8. *London Calling* – The Clash

9. *Blonde on Blonde* – Bob Dylan

10. *The Beatles* (The White Album) – The Beatles

11. *The Sun Sessions* – Elvis Presley

12. *Kind of Blue* – Miles Davis

13. *The Velvet Underground and Nico* – The Velvet Underground

14. *Abbey Road* – The Beatles

15. *Are You Experienced?* – The Jimi Hendrix Experience

16. *Blood on the Tracks* – Bob Dylan

17. *Nevermind* – Nirvana

18. *Born to Run* – Bruce Springsteen

19. *Astral Weeks* – Van Morrison

20. *Thriller* – Michael Jackson

THE 10 BEST-SELLING SINGLES OF ALL TIME

1. "Candle in the Wind (Princess Diana Tribute)" – Elton John **(37 million sold)**

2. "White Christmas" – Bing Crosby **(30 million)**

3. "Rock Around the Clock" – Bill Haley and His Comets **(17 million)**

4. "I Want to Hold Your Hand" – The Beatles **(12 million)**

5. "Hey Jude" – The Beatles **(10 million)**

6. "It's Now or Never" – Elvis Presley **(10 million)**

7. "I Will Always Love You" – Whitney Houston **(10 million)**

8. "Hound Dog" – Elvis Presley **(9 million)**

9. "Diana" – Paul Anka **(9 million)**

10. "(Everything I Do) I Do It for You" – Bryan Adams **(8 million)**

ROCK STARS YOU'VE NEVER HEARD OF

Aviv Geffen

Scion of a famous Israeli family—his uncle is the military leader Moshe Dayan, while his father is the famous left-wing poet and journalist Yohonatan Geffen—Aviv Geffen is one of Israel's biggest stars.

In 1995, aged just 18, Aviv became famous all over the Middle East when he sang at the same Tel Aviv Peace Rally where former Israeli Labour Party leader and Nobel Peace Prize winner Yitzhak Rabin was assassinated by gunmen. Now a fantastic, goth-rock amalgam of David Bowie, Prince, and Bob Dylan, Geffen has released 10 albums in the last 13 years, most recently with his band, the Mistakes.

"Shir Hatikvah" (Song of Hope) is classic Geffen with the lyrics: "We'll bury our guns/And not our children/We'll take over the peace/And not territories."

"The world's eyes are looking at Israel," Geffen said recently. "I'm here to support the peace process and respect the Arabs."

gods of rock

FIRST-EVER STADIUM ROCK SHOW

On August 15, 1965, pop music made its epochal move from theaters to sports stadiums when the Beatles played in front of 53,275 people at their first show at Shea Stadium, the home of the New York Mets.

A huge police cordon was placed between the Beatles and the fans, whose screaming reached such a peak that the band spent almost the entire concert unable to hear a note they played. Thanks to their use of the baseball park's frankly awful in-house PA system, none of the fans could hear them, either, and were thus robbed of enjoying John Lennon playing an electric keyboard with his elbow and talking to himself in some secret, made-up language. The Beatles were supported by King Curtis, Brenda Holloway, Sounds Incorporated, and the Discotheque Dancers.

A few weeks after the show, Lennon made remarks to the *Evening Standard* about the Beatles being bigger than Jesus and the American Midwest began to turn on the band. The band would return to Shea Stadium a year later and play their last-ever stadium show on August 29, 1966, at Candlestick Park in San Francisco.

> **When I was a Beatle I thought we were the best group in the goddamn world, and believing that is what made us what we were.**
> John Lennon

> **I want to go out at the top, but the secret is knowing when you're at the top, it's so difficult in this business, your career fluctuates all the time, up and down, like a pair of trousers.**
>
> Rod Stewart

THE LONGEST CONCERT — WILL IT EVER END?

The Grand Boys formed in Scotland in 1990 with the sole intention of raising money for charity. To date, they have collected in excess of $285,000 for a wide variety of causes.

The band comprises Paul Bromley (drums, bass); John Griffin (guitar, vocals); Bob Kelly (lead guitar, bass, whistle, vocals); Robert Kelly (lead guitar, bass, vocals); Alan Marshall (guitar); Adrian Robertson (bass, lead guitar, vocals); Colin Sinclair (accordion); and Alan Stewart (drums).

So far, so good. However, could you imagine wanting to watch *any* band for more than, say, a few hours? Well, at Smith's Restaurant in Stirling in February 2004, the Grand Boys, who play a mixture of folk, country and western, and rock 'n' roll, played for a world-record time of 42 hours, 38 minutes. "It was a long, hard slog which left us with sore fingers, no voice and extremely tired," said the band members later.

The group appropriately opened their record-breaking marathon concert with the number "Dedication," the theme tune to the classic BBC TV show *Record Breakers*, as written and performed by the late great presenter and all-round entertainer Roy Castle.

THE WORST BAND – EVER

In August 2003, the US rock magazine *Blender* ran a writers' poll to find the worst band of all time. All the usual suspects were in there—the Doors, Vanilla Ice, Starship, etc.—but one band garnered more votes than any other, and that was numb-brained Detroit rap metal duo Insane Clown Posse (ICP). They are known for their schlocky face paint, crassly violent lyrics, and crappy stage antics—a favorite for some years has been soaking their fans, known as Juggalos, with a drink called Faygo, a cheap fizzy soda available in over 50 flavors. ICP have enjoyed laughable spats with Eminem while attempting to out-merchandise even credit-card legends KISS. In 2002, the band revealed their "secret message" was to follow God and make it to heaven.

> **We want to be the band to dance to when the bomb drops.**
> Simon Le Bon

TRY FITTING THIS ALBUM TITLE ON YOUR IPOD

The album with the longest title to chart in the USA contains no less than 90 words. The album is from New York's Fiona Apple and was released on November 9, 1999. Here it is:

When the Pawn Hits the Conflicts He Thinks Like a King, What He Knows Throws the Blows When He Goes to the Fight, and He'll Win the Whole Thing 'Fore He Enters the Ring, There's No Body to Batter When Your Mind Is Your Might, So When You Go Solo You Hold Your Own Hand, and Remember That Depth Is the Greatest of Heights, and If You Know Where You Stand, Then You'll Know Where to Land, and If You Fall It Won't Matter, Cuz You'll Know That You're Right.

ANOTHER UNKNOWN

Ammar Hassan

Palestinian Ammar Hassan became a Muslim sensation when he came second in the 13-week *Superstar 2* competition held on the Lebanese TV channel al-Mustaqbal during the summer of 2004.

Deep-voiced Hassan's battle with the "cute" Libyan contestant Ayman al-Aathar drove the show toward its massive ratings success while stunts like flying the pair to Tripoli to meet Colonel Gaddafi only accentuated the air of insanity. Gaddafi—who always backed the Palestinian—was later reported to have sung a song with the wannabe stars.

Hassan, originally from the northern West Bank town of Salfit, has lived in the United Arab Emirates for five years now, but, rather like Clay Aiken in an Islamic scarf, he's gone on to far outstrip his winning rival. His appearances have become legendary for the emotions they provoke.

During a recent show in the West Bank city of Nablus, dozens of masked and armed men stormed a concert by Hassan, setting fire to tires and starting chants against the singer. However, Hassan wasn't rattled; just 45 minutes later, with order restored, he reopened his show with a song praising "Holy Jerusalem," a move that many thought was an effort to soothe the armed men still in the audience.

Less than an hour later, armed guards whisked Hassan off stage for his own safety. A lesson for all pop stars there.

We should all commit suicide at 45.
Roger Daltrey

gods of rock

OVERRATED ALBUMS

Here are five of the most overrated albums of all time, as voted in 1998's Rock and Roll Poll of Polls, drawn from 20,000 votes cast in the UK and US.

Brothers in Arms – Dire Straits:
"Grumbly"

Rumours – Fleetwood Mac:
"Airy-fairy"

Hotel California – The Eagles:
"Drug-addled"

Bat Out of Hell – Meat Loaf:
"Theatrical"

Bridge Over Troubled Water – Simon and Garfunkel:
"Overblown"

THE ONE-HIT WONDER THAT REFUSES TO DIE

"Right Here, Right Now" – Jesus Jones (1991)

One night back in 1990, Mike Edwards, front man and singer for Jesus Jones, wrote "Right Here, Right Now." The band released it as a single in 1991 and watched, with no small pleasure, as it soared to the top of the US charts. The song still pays its way 15 years later, appearing on jukeboxes and karaoke CDs. Modest payments would accrue here and there, but it wasn't until the band's website alerted Edwards to a new group of consumers eager to use the song that the real cash arrived.

Already on tour in America ("A spartan trip compared with our old days," Edwards revealed), playing five shows a week, a corporate management conference wanted to book the band to play three shows at a five-star Florida resort and were offering all expenses paid and "multiples" of the profit the band would make on the tour.

Each "show"—one night in every three—was in a sense an abbreviated show: "Right Here, Right Now" played twice. About four minutes' work. The band went home after 10 days with more money than they'd seen for years.

PLEASE TURN IT DOWN: THE LOUDEST BAND IN THE WORLD

Some 20 years ago, Manowar made a promise to fans planning to come and see them live. That promise was: "We will melt your face!" It wasn't a promise they made lightly.

Existing on the fringes of metal, where theatricality, baby oil and Tarzan-like chamois leather Y-fronts are entirely acceptable, Manowar came together to produce an act so camp and hilarious that much of the adolescent world fell at their feet. After signing their record contract in blood, the band released a stream of ever more ludicrously overblown LPs ("Hail to England" was a favorite), but in 1992, in Hanover, Germany, they peaked. One "facemelting" gig was measured at 129.5 decibels, sent through 10 tons of amplifiers and speakers 40 ft long and 21 ft high.

The band is still touring and remains the live act most Russian music fans would like to see, well above the Beatles and Michael Jackson.

THE FIRST NUMBER 1 ALBUM

Already huge stars at clubs and theaters, in films, and on radio all across America, Nat King Cole's jazz and swing trio had hit after hit on the Black Music Chart during the mid-1940s. But when Capitol released *The King Cole Trio*—four 78 rpm discs containing eight tracks—as their debut album proper in the autumn of 1944, the collection sold like no other.

When *Billboard* magazine created its first album chart on March 24, 1945, *The King Cole Trio* was right there at number 1. And it wouldn't—or couldn't—be shifted for 12 weeks. What made the record's success all the more amazing was that big-band and swing music was declining in popularity as jazz fans became turned on to the all-new sounds of bebop. Ironically, for all its success, *The King Cole Trio* album marked the beginning of the end of jazz as a mainstream-pleasing and truly popular style of music.

SPIN MAGAZINE'S 20 GREATEST BANDS

In 2002, *Spin* magazine compiled a list of 50 great bands from the 1960s forward. According to *Spin*: "To qualify, these groups had to have a roof-raising, history-changing sound, presence or hairstyle. They also had to clearly influence today's music in undeniable ways." Here are their top 20:

1. The Beatles

2. The Ramones

3. Led Zeppelin

4. Bob Marley and the Wailers

5. Nirvana

6. Parliament/Funkadelic

7. The Clash

8. Public Enemy

9. The Rolling Stones

10. Beastie Boys

11. The Velvet Underground

12. Sly and the Family Stone

13. U2

14. Run DMC

15. Radiohead

16. The Jimi Hendrix Experience

17. Sonic Youth

18. AC/DC

19. The Stooges

20. Metallica

AN UNLIKELY FEMALE POP SINGER

A 25-year-old Manhattan resident wants to be a famous pop singer. Wafah Dufour is certainly sexy enough, her slim figure, full lips, and dark and sultry look perfectly complementing her top-drawer, Fifth Avenue style. She sings in English and has a clearly defined Western style, but Dufour's having a hard time getting people to listen and she thinks her uncle Osama might be to blame.

You see, until recently, Dufour was known as Wafah bin Laden. Her estranged father is Bin Laden's half brother, and ever since Osama's men flew those planes into the Twin Towers, young Wafah's career has been stalled at the starting line. How selfish of him.

In 2005, Dufour appeared on US talk show *The Big Night* and revealed that she had been raised by her mother since she was 10 and has no contact whatsoever with other parts of the family.

"It's hard to answer these questions," she complained. "I just want people in the States to know I have nothing to do with that person and it's hard for me to be always associated with him. It's a big family and I don't know what everybody else has done."

Now tell us you wouldn't love to see her video on MTV.

> **All we had ever heard about record company people is that they were vampires and criminals and they killed Elvis Presley.**
> Bjork

MOST PSEUDONONYMOUS POP STAR

Rather surprisingly, John Lennon is the pop star who has recorded under the most pseudonyms, as claimed by *Guinness Book of World Records*. The Beatle recorded and produced music under no less than 15 different names.

Some of the names that Lennon used included: The Honorary John St. John Johnson, The Rev. Fred Ghurkin, Dr. Winston O'Ghurkin, Dwarf McDougal, Dr. Winston O'Boogie, Rev. Thumbs Ghurkin, Kaptain Kundalini, Mel Torment, Dr. Dream, Dr. Winston O'Reggae, John O'Cean, Beatcomber, and Johnny Silver.

Most of these names appeared on the cover of 1974's *Walls and Bridges* album.

Suffice to say, Lennon was drinking fairly heavily at the time.

HAVE YOU HEARD OF THIS ONE?

Utada Hikaru

Virtually unknown outside of her native Japan, 22-year-old Hikaru, known as Hikki, is her country's biggest pop star. Beloved of the Japanese media, a typical Hikaru headline used to be: "Bilingual straight-A student and the diva of the Heisei Period" (i.e. the the diva of the modern age). Hikaru's work is devoured by the Japanese public like no one before her. Her debut CD, *First Love* (1999), sold more than nine million copies—it remains the best-selling album in Japanese history. Not too bad for the then 16-year-old.

While Japanese pop is consistently overwhelmed by baby-talking nonentities, Hikaru likes to flaunt her love of everything from Metallica to the hottest US R&B CD (she's worked with N*E*R*D and Darkchild) and remains defiantly angsty. She launched herself as Hikaru Utada, the English version of her name, in America in 2004.

Musical activism

activism

A GLANCE AT THOSE WHO LIKE TO MIX
THEIR POLITICS WITH THEIR POP

In 1984, former Boomtown Rat Bob Geldof and his pal Midge Ure (formerly of 1970s monk-attired pop sensations Slik, and then moody synth types Ultravox) saw footage of people starving in Ethiopia and decided to do something. They wrote the biggest-selling record of all time (until it was topped by Elton John's Princess Diana eulogy, "Candle in the Wind") and in 1985 organized the biggest concert of all time, Live Aid.

Live Aid had the unforeseen side effect of reinvigorating the careers of the likes of Status Quo, and cementing Phil Collins's fame (he flew on the Concorde directly after performing at the Wembley Live Aid concert to appear at the Philadelphia concert). But it did raise an awful lot of money and awareness.

However, some 20 years later, there was still famine in Africa, which was especially rife in Niger, and so Geldof and Ure organized Live 8, this time an overtly political concert aimed at influencing the leaders of the G8, who were meeting in Edinburgh in 2005 to discuss canceling the debts that have helped to cripple the economies of developing countries. Concerts were held all over the world, and stars such as Paul McCartney, Sting, Coldplay, U2, Bjork, and the reformed Pink Floyd all performed.

Several days after the concert, London was attacked by suicide bombers, which meant the impact of the Live 8 concerts (as well as the celebration of London being awarded the 2012 Olympics) was short-lived. The day after the bombings, the Drop the Debt campaign described the debt relief agreements reached at the G8 meeting as: "no giant leap."

> **As a rock star, I have two instincts, I want to have fun, and I want to change the world.**
> Bono

SONGS USED FOR POLITICAL CAMPAIGNS

"Things Can Only Get Better" – D:Ream
Endlessly hammered by Britain's Labour Party at every opportunity
in their attempt to oust the Tories in 1997.

"Beautiful Day" – U2
Used by Labour in their 2005 campaign.

"Right Here, Right Now" – Fatboy Slim
Used by Labour in 2004 for the conference and for a by-election. Slim was
not happy. "I am anti-war and I don't trust Blair," he said. "I don't want
anyone to think that I support him."

"Don't Stop" – Fleetwood Mac
This 1970s soft rock classic was used by Bill Clinton as part of his 1992
campaign. Which he won.

"Rock 'n' Roll Part Two" – Gary Glitter
Used by George Bush to heighten excitement at rallies. The tune was
dropped when someone pointed out Gary's jail sentence for child porn.

"New Beginning" – Boyzone
This was the Liberal Democrats' song for the 2001 election. Oh dear.

**We don't comment on whales and the
rainforest. We don't try to be
ambassadors to Bosnia. You need a
rock star for that? Some idiot who
couldn't tune a guitar six months ago
is now an environmental expert?**
Gene Simmons, KISS

gods of rock

ONE LOVE

In the 1970s, few countries had a more dangerous political landscape than Jamaica. The Jamaican prime minister was Michael Manley, a socialist and close friend of Fidel Castro. His party, the People's National Party (PNP), supported several of Jamaica's street gangs, as did the opposition Jamaica Labour Party (JLP). Voter intimidation and the display of power were part and parcel of Jamaican elections.

The island's music scene was intimately bound up with its political life, and as Jamaica's most famous son, Bob Marley was eagerly sought out to voice support for the PNP. He agreed to perform at a free concert organized by the PNP in the run-up to the 1976 election. Days before the election, armed men raided Marley's home and started shooting. Marley was shot in the arm and chest and his wife, Rita, was injured from a shot to the head. Police never caught the gunmen, although it was widely thought to be the work of one of the street gangs sponsored by the JLP. During the 1980 election, 800 people died as a result of political violence. In 1980, Marley's role as an important figure in world politics was underlined when he played a festival to celebrate Zimbabwe's independence.

COLDPLAY

Just when it seemed that bands talking about politics was out of fashion forever, along came Coldplay who, as soon as they became unassailably popular, started campaigning on a number of issues, particularly free trade. They've turned down multimillion-dollar offers from companies like Coca-Cola with the eye-raising comment: "It's a lot of money, but we have more than we need."

When they were first approached about fair trade by Oxfam, the band's reaction was "Fair what?" but since then, they have used the merchandise booth on their tours to gather signatures for Oxfam's fair trade petition. They have gathered some 30,000 names, and lead singer Chris Martin has met with the World Trade Organization to deliver a petition of four million names.

When he started his activism, Martin said: "I feel like a third-rate Bono. Hopefully it'll escalate until I feel like a full-on Bono."

The Beatles, as ever, blazed a trail through politics in their own way. They were the first pop stars to be afforded any respect from the political establishment when Britain's Prime Minister Harold Wilson awarded the Fab Four OBEs in 1965. Lennon famously returned his a few years later, protesting at the escalation of the Vietnam War and "Cold Turkey" slipping down the charts.

Lennon's political activism in the 1970s put him on the watch list of the US government and in particular Richard Nixon. The CIA saw him as an undesirable alien thanks to his preaching revolution, leading marches in the company of activists such as Jerry Rubin, and plans to hold a "revolutionary road show," a series of concerts with anti-Nixon, anti-Vietnam speakers that would travel across the USA, climaxing with a rally at the Republican convention. The government feared a showdown between themselves and America's youth, and so set about disarming Lennon by tangling him up in court cases fighting for his right to remain resident in the US. The process drained Lennon's political energy and dampened his enthusiasm for causing trouble.

But the political controversy badge doesn't solely belong to Lennon. Paul McCartney had his moment when his single "Give Ireland Back to the Irish" was banned by the BBC. He responded by making his next release as inoffensive as possible: "Mary Had a Little Lamb."

> **We're out for one thing only, and that's to bring back the resurgence of Black Power.**
>
> Chuck D., Public Enemy

NOT EXACTLY SUPPORTIVE SONGS ABOUT MARGARET THATCHER

"Stand Down Margaret" – The Beat

"Tramp the Dirt Down" – Elvis Costello

"Waiting for the Great Leap Forwards" – Billy Bragg

"Two Million Voices" – Angelic Upstarts

"Taking Tea with Pinochet" – Christy Moore

"Margaret on the Guillotine" – Morrissey

"Black Boys on Mopeds" – Sinead O'Connor

"Get Your Filthy Hands Off My Desert" – Pink Floyd

"Don't Pay the Poll Tax" – The Exploited

COOL BRITANNIA

In 1997, after 18 years of Tory rule, Labour won the general election. After the music-hating Tories, a Labour government was greeted with a sigh of relief by many a British music star. The victory coincided with the rise of Britpop, a confluence of British pop groups of the ilk of Oasis, Blur, and Pulp, all of whom were drawing tabloid headlines in a manner not seen since the likes of the Beatles and the Rolling Stones in the 1960s. Within two months of forming Britain's new government, Prime Minister Tony Blair (who had the distinction of being the first British prime minister to have played guitar in a band—Ugly Rumours they were called—when he was in college) held a summer champagne reception to which he invited Noel Gallagher, Creation Records boss Alan McGee, and Mick Hucknall of Simply Red.

Within two years, the relationship had soured. Alan McGee called Tony Blair a control freak and withdrew his financial support (he'd donated $89,000 before the election); Noel Gallagher described himself as an "idiot" for getting drawn into what he considered to be a publicity stunt on behalf of Tony Blair. In 2001, Culture Secretary Tessa Jowell described Labour's Cool Britannia project as having "missed the point."

> **I'm like Mayor of America right now. I could probably run for President.**
> Ice-T

THE ANARCHISTS

Chumbawamba
Anarcho-syndicalist punks who lived in a commune and signed to EMI Records with whom they enjoyed international success with the drinking song "Tubthumping." They once tipped a bucket of water over Deputy Prime Minister John Prescott at an awards ceremony.

Crass
Anarcho-syndicalist punk rockers who lived in a commune and released DIY records of livid political diatribes throughout the 1980s.

Flux of Pink Indians
The band formed by the owner of One Little Indian (the record label that gave us Bjork) who were very into animal rights and the ideals of anarchism.

Fugazi
Anarcho-syndicalist punk band, whose stripped-down music and lifestyle gave birth to a straight-edge phenomenon of abstinence. Adherents do not drink, take drugs, or eat meat.

Sex Pistols
Not anarcho-syndicalist at all, but certainly made anarchy a fashionable idea among many punks with their stirring anthem "Anarchy in the UK." The Pistols' brand of anarchy could be better described as chaos.

RED WEDGE

After the second Conservative election victory in 1983, things were looking very bleak indeed for Britain's lefties. Margaret Thatcher was running roughshod over the unions, the miners, and the youth. She was riding a wave of post–Falklands War euphoria. It was not a good time to be young.

In an attempt to gather support for the ailing Labour opposition in the run-up to the 1987 general election, Red Wedge was formed by Billy Bragg, Paul Weller (who, during his first flush of success in the 1970s, had come out as a Tory supporter), and Communard Jimmy Somerville. Red Wedge organized concert tours in the UK with appearances by the likes of Jerry Dammers (formerly of the Specials), Madness, Prefab Sprout, and the Smiths. Not everyone was won over by Red Wedge (not least the electorate, which returned a Conservative government for a third term in 1987). Joe Strummer of the Clash, for example, said: "I don't want to slag Red Wedge off, I don't want to go up against the firing squad, but if I was true to myself, I'd have to say that I find it a little boring."

Having failed to topple the Tory government, Red Wedge was disbanded in 1990, an event that might have prompted Billy Bragg's manager, Pete Jenner, to comment ruefully: "If you have a good, right-on cause, don't ask Billy to play a benefit for it, because you'll lose." The same might be said of the Blow Monkeys, a once very popular band who released no less than five anti-Thatcher singles during the run-up to the 1987 election and even had one of them banned until the election was finished.

It's ridiculous to suggest we are involved with fascists. All my best friends are black, gay, Irish or criminals.

Johnny Rotten

> **When you're as rich as I am, you don't have to be political.**
>
> Sting

MEANWHILE, IN AMERICA

Margaret Thatcher's counterpart in America was the former actor Ronald Reagan. His two terms in office ended in 1989, and he was succeeded by George Bush.

Twelve years of right-wing Republicanism resulted in few high-profile rock 'n' roll voices of dissent, but one of the loudest was that of Rage Against the Machine. They emerged in 1990, and with their mix of rap and hard rock would go on to become a major influence on the multimillion-selling nu-metal scene, which spawned some of the world's biggest-selling acts such as Linkin Park and Nine Inch Nails.

While Rage Against the Machine were concerned with many issues, their best-known moment of political protest came in 1993 when they were playing the Lollapalooza Festival in Philadelphia. In an anti-censorship stunt aimed largely at the PMRC (Parents Music Resource Center), they appeared on stage entirely naked, their mouths covered in tape, and stood still for 15 minutes. The only music was the sound of their guitars feeding back. In another episode, shortly before the group disbanded in 2000, they shot a video for their single "Sleep Now in the Fire" with well-known political activist and filmmaker Michael Moore directing. It was shot outside the New York Stock Exchange. The chaos the filming caused forced the Stock Exchange to close an hour early, thus striking a small blow against the mighty monolith of capitalism.

Less well known but possibly even more angry than Rage Against the Machine were Consolidated, a band who dubbed themselves a "white, Marxist Public Enemy." Their gigs, which were a punishing mixture of very loud and brutal beats and intense political diatribes, were usually followed by pass-the-mike Q&A sessions that would regularly descend into shouting matches between dreadlocked vegan punk activists and drunk frat boys.

gods of rock

MC5

In the radical late 1960s, it was Detroit's MC5 (Motor City Five) who were the revolutionary punks of choice. They were the house band of the White Panther Party, a revolutionary political collective formed by John Sinclair (who was also MC5's manager) in 1968. The Panthers' political platform demanded the ending of capitalism, via a total assault on the cultural life of America using rock 'n' roll, drugs, and sex. From the beginning, the White Panthers and MC5 were considered a serious threat to political stability in America. One of the Panthers' co-founders, Lawrence (Pun) Plamondon, was arrested in connection with the bombing of a CIA office in Ann Arbor. Despite the fact that the band did little more than play some hard, basic rock 'n' roll, influenced by early Rolling Stones and the Who, they were singled out by Vice President Spiro Agnew in his Commission on Terrorism and the New Left as part of a possible North Vietnamese plot to bring America to its knees by embroiling its youth in promiscuity and drug addiction. Government harassment of the band reached its climax when John Sinclair was given a 10-year jail sentence for selling two joints to an undercover police officer. John Lennon played at a rally in his defense. MC5 broke up in 1972, leaving an incendiary musical (and revolutionary) legacy that later inspired the Sex Pistols and the Clash.

To say politics and music don't mix is to say that politics and gardening don't mix, or politics and plumbing. Politics concerns everybody.

Chris Martin

MUSICAL FIGURES WHO RAN FOR ELECTION

Altern 8
Chris Peat of the madcap acid house group started the Altern8ive (Hardcore) Party and ran in the 1992 election in Stafford. He polled 178 votes (0.3percent of the total).

Coldcut
The band started their own political party for the 2001 election, called The Guilty Party.

Malcolm McLaren
In 1999, the former Sex Pistols manager announced he was going to run for London mayor. He proposed that libraries should have bars, brothels should be legalized, and trams reintroduced to the streets of London. He pulled out of the election, which was eventually won by Ken Livingstone, a man who had his own moment of rock fame when he provided guest narration on the track "Arnold Same" on the Blur album *Great Escape*.

Screaming Lord Sutch
First ran as a candidate for the National Teenage Party in Stratford-upon-Avon in 1963 and polled 209 votes. He ran again against Harold Wilson in 1966 in Huyton and received 585 votes. The Monster Raving Loony Party was established in 1983.

PUNKS AND SONNY RUNNING FOR OFFICE

Jello Biafra (born Eric Boucher), singer of the Californian punk gods the Dead Kennedys and anti-censorship middle America baiter, is a political animal first and foremost. To prove his point, he ran for mayor in San Francisco in 1987. He got himself a respectable haircut, donned a suit, and came in 4th out of 10 candidates.

Sonny Bono, famous for being married to Cher and the smash hit "I Got You Babe," ran for election as mayor in Palm Springs, California, mainly because he wanted to open a restaurant and found the planning application process too onerous. He won and eventually became elected to the US House of Representatives in 1994 as a Republican. His main contribution to American life was to extend copyright protection after the death of the copyright owner from 50 to 70 years (and from 70 to 95 years for corporate copyright).

WHAT'S GOING ON?

In 1971, Marvin Gaye released what is still considered by many to be the best soul album ever made: *What's Going On* Marvin's brother, Frankie, had just returned from a tour of duty in Vietnam, and the stories he had to tell inspired in Gaye a new political edge. The album concerned itself with all manner of political topics—the state of the planet, racism, and inequality in America, the war in Vietnam—but all delivered with a sweetness that empowered the album's political punch by dint of its huge popularity.

When he delivered the finished album to Motown, the label's owner, Berry Gordy, was horrified. He knew that prior to recording the album, Gaye had been devastated by the death of his duet partner Tammi Terrell, and that he had become increasingly wayward, thanks to his drug use. Gordy thought the album was too political to sell and initially refused to release it. However, he eventually gave in, and the album delivered Motown three hit singles and went on to become one of the most highly regarded albums the label ever released.

BONO

Bono seems to relish his role as an activist as much as he does being a pop star. Indeed, it seems that the pop star part of the equation is now being fueled in order to maintain his profile as an activist.

In 2002, he accompanied US Treasury Secretary Paul O'Neill on a tour of African countries, and he set up DATA (Debt, Aids, Trade in Africa) to raise awareness of these issues. He bullied the Canadian prime minister over his sluggishness in raising Canada's aid to Africa and even met with George W. Bush privately.

Afterward, Bono appeared on the lawn of the White House with Bush and endorsed the president's plans for world aid. He was also mentioned as a possible candidate for the president of the World Bank.

Maybe, though, he took the politics/music game a bit too far when he described Tony Blair and Chancellor Gordon Brown as "the John and Paul of the global development stage." Bono is smart enough to know, however, that he is "the worst scourge on God's green earth; a rock star with a cause."

The drugs don't work

BOOZERS, LOSERS, AND SUBSTANCE ABUSERS

AN OBJECT LESSON IN SELF-DESTRUCTION — KEITH MOON

Frankly, the Who's drummer Keith Moon should never have been allowed to walk past an open bar, never mind be floated into a world of insane drug and alcohol abuse on the fat clouds of his own brilliance. Some people know when to stop, but Moon never stopped. Already a star by his late teens, the drummer used alcohol, pills, and cocaine to support his "madman" image. Never allowed to be "off," Moon had to drink more, snort more, eat more pills, and act more aggressively and stupidly than everyone else. He actually drove a car into a swimming pool on his 21st birthday; stripped naked in airports and on television shows; destroyed hotel rooms; swung from chandeliers; threw televisions out of hotel windows; put cherry bombs in toilets; and left his own personal hovercraft on train tracks. He died in 1978 from an overdose of anti-alcoholism drugs in the same Mayfair apartment where Mama Cass had died four years previously.

10 SONGS ABOUT HEROIN

"King Heroin" — James Brown
"Jane Said" — Jane's Addiction
"Cold Turkey" — John Lennon
"Comfortably Numb" — Pink Floyd
"Dead Flowers" — The Rolling Stones
"White Lady Loves You More" — Elliott Smith
"Cop Shoot Cop" — Spiritualized
"Golden Brown" — The Stranglers
"Heroin" — The Velvet Underground
"The Needle and the Damage Done" — Neil Young

At our peak, we did more drugs, had more groupies and threw wilder parties than Led Zeppelin.
Glenn Frey, the Eagles

SONGS ABOUT COCAINE

"Cocaine" – J. J. Cale/Eric Clapton
"Cocaine" – Jackson Browne
"Cocaine Blues" – Johnny Cash
"Cocaine Business" – Noreaga
"Cocaine Eyes" – Neil Young
"Glamour Profession" – Steely Dan
"Wacky Dust" – Ella Fitzgerald and Chuck Web
"Invisible Touch" – Genesis
"Moonlight Mile" – The Rolling Stones
"(What's the Story) Morning Glory" – Oasis
"Night of the Living Bassheads" – Public Enemy
"Snowblind" – Black Sabbath
"Snowblind" – Styx
"Snow Blind Friend" – Steppenwolf
"Sometimes I Rhyme Slow" – Nice and Smooth
"White Lines" – Grandmaster Flash and Melle Mel
"Witchy Woman" – The Eagles

SPEED DEMONS

Amphetamines have been restricted to prescription use only since 1970, but sometimes the need to keep going when your body is screaming at you to stop is unavoidable. A teenage Jerry Lee Lewis used to be tipped in Benzedrine capsules in bars across the southern states. Johnny Cash and the Everly Brothers had serious speed habits, while country legend Hank Williams pilled himself to death aged 29.

The Beatles gobbled Preludin, "Prellies," by the handful in Hamburg in order to play for hours, seven nights a week, but it was the Mods, in debt to black American soul and Italian tailoring, who defined amphetamine use in the mid-1960s. Strange, then, that probably the last genuine rock star to still be quoted as favoring amphetamines is Motorhead's Ian "Lemmy" Kilminster, whose cowboy-boot, black-denim, and belt-buckle look is about as far from the Mod aesthetic as is possible.

RED HOT CHILI PEPPERS

Brought up by a small-time TV actor and drug dealer father who introduced him to Alice Cooper, Led Zeppelin, and the Who's Keith Moon, Anthony Kiedis was drinking, snorting coke, and smoking marijuana from a young age, before moving on to heroin and crack. Not exactly a well-balanced diet, but one that fueled Kiedis and bandmate Hillel Slovak from the mid-1980s until the latter's death in 1988, an event that precipitated a series of huge drug binges. Kiedis set about attempting to drain the world dry of drugs, spending weeks at a time holed up in his LA mansion shooting cocaine to go up and heroin to come down. Meanwhile, new guitarist John Frusciante was holed up in *his* LA mansion doing the same thing, except he would stay there shooting drugs until his hair, teeth, and nails fell out. Kiedis cleaned up and relapsed three times, but finally got clean for good in 2000. Read his book *Scar Tissue,* and you'll wonder how he ever survived.

WEED OUT THE TROUBLEMAKERS

Marijuana was in Bob Marley's blood in more ways than one. An uncle was in a rural Quadrille (think of it as Jamaican bluegrass) band, and their appetite for booze and weed was legendary. But it was Bob himself who would transport the concept of reggae, Rastafarianism, and marijuana as a healing herb to a worldwide audience.

Although, as a major rock star of the 1970s, he was regularly offered cocaine and LSD, Marley only ever smoked weed, and his influence, alongside that of bandmate Peter Tosh, sealed forever the image of the dreadlock Rasta wreathed in thick blue-gray smoke. Marley, like massively popular Jamaican DJs U-Roy, Yabby You, and Yellowman, regularly hymned praise to marijuana, even appearing on the *Kaya* album sparking a fat joint. The word *kaya* is also a Jamaican word for "cannabis."

Writer Harry Shapiro—using evidence from interviews and reports during Marley's lifetime—has estimated that between 1966 and his death in 1980, Marley consumed somewhere around 650 lbs of the finest weed his country had to offer, making him a true African Herbsman.

CITY POISON

In 1966, artist Andy Warhol created a traveling show called the Exploding Plastic Inevitable that featured a band called the Velvet Underground. Their music was the sound of the death of the hippie dream; their drugs of choice, speed, and heroin. Violent ups, violent downs. The epitome of nihilistic New York City cool, the Velvets would flesh out live versions of "Heroin," and "Waiting for the Man." But while band leader Lou Reed would always be ambivalent about his drug use, their influence was enormous. In the early 1970s, the New York Dolls took the baton and ran with it until most of them were dead. Pills and booze killed their first drummer; guitarist Johnny Thunders would regularly pawn his instrument for smack, and tours were canceled when the dope failed to arrive. The band's new English manager was Malcom McLaren. When, in 1975, he failed to kick-start their career, he formed a new band back in London called the Sex Pistols. The music was fresh, but the drugs the fans favored, the barbiturates, heroin, and speed, were the same as ever.

SLY STONE

Texas born and from a deeply religious background, Sly Stone started out good but turned oh, so very bad. He started as the leader of Sly and the Family Stone, a group of amiable, multiracial hippie-funk musicians in San Francisco in 1967. When the band took off, Sly was put under pressure by the Black Panther movement to hire more black musicians. The stress led to ulcers, which led to prescription drugs. Then cocaine and phencyclidine (PCP) took hold, and soon the band was more interested in partying than playing (helped, no doubt, by Stone's insistence on carrying a violin case filled with cocaine wherever he went). Between summer 1969 and autumn 1971—the peak of the band's fame—only one double-A-side single, "Thank You (Falettinme Be Mice Elf Again)/Everybody Is a Star," was released. The band's career nose-dived, and when they split in 1974, Sly sank into serious drug abuse, at one point addicted to PCP. Sly entered drug addiction counseling in 1984. In 1987, he was arrested for cocaine possession and use. A Sly and the Family Stone tribute album, *Different Strokes by Different Folks*, has recently been released.

gods of rock

TOO MUCH TOO YOUNG: SUBSTANCE DEATHS

Billy Murcia (New York Dolls) – 21 (drugs)

Sid Vicious (Sex Pistols) – 21 (heroin)

Robbie McIntosh (Average White Band) – 24 (heroin)

Kristen Pfaff (Hole) – 24 (heroin)

Tommy Bolin (Deep Purple) – 25 (heroin)

James Honeyman-Scott (Pretenders) – 25 (heroin)

Hillel Slovak (Red Hot Chili Peppers) – 26 (heroin)

Jimi Hendrix – 27 (heroin)

Janis Joplin – 27 (heroin)

Tim Buckley – 28 (heroin)

Danny Whitten (Crazy Horse) – 29 (heroin)

John Bonham (Led Zeppelin) – 32 (alcohol)

Bon Scott (AC/DC) – 33 (alcohol)

Jonathan Melvoin (Smashing Pumpkins) – 34 (heroin)

Johnny Thunders (New York Dolls) – 38 (heroin)

David Ruffin (Temptations) – 50 (drugs)

> **I've always needed a drug to survive. The others, too, but I always had more, more pills, more of everything because I'm more crazy, probably.**
> John Lennon

PAUL MCCARTNEY: HOW TO DO DRUGS PROPERLY

Some rock stars are more sensible than others. Take Sir Paul. In his mid-20s he was introduced to cocaine but, unlike so many others, he tired of it very rapidly. "I did cocaine for about a year around the time of *Sgt. Pepper*," he has said. "Coke and maybe some grass to balance it out. I was never completely crazy with cocaine. I'd been introduced to it and at first it seemed OK, like anything that's new and stimulating . . . but it got too fashionable, *too* fashionable, darling, amongst the record execs. I couldn't handle all that, being in the bogs with all those creeps!"

Perhaps a little foolishly, McCartney tried to get almost half a pound of pot into Japan in January 1980 and was busted and briefly jailed, but apart from that, he's never had a problem, never needed treatment, never been named and shamed. A hero, a knight of the realm, a beacon, if you like, for sensible moderation.

In 2004, he revealed that he had tried heroin at the height of the Beatles' success. "I didn't realize I'd taken it," he told *Uncut* magazine. "It didn't do anything for me."

KEITH RICHARDS

Keith Richards annoys people for the very fact he's still alive. How has he managed it? How has he spent the last 40-odd years doing enormous quantities of drugs, chain-smoking, and drinking pints of vodka and orange, and only have the world's most lived-in face to show for it? In 1967, Keith was dabbling with pot, LSD, and speed. By the early 1970s, he was a globally glamorous junkie, his crow's-nest stack of hair the only thing moving as he nodded out backstage. Richards has been busted, jailed, nearly fired from the band, and yet, as Barbara Charone wrote in her 1979 biography of the Stones' guitarist, it's always music that saves him. When he's not playing live, when he's away from the relentless demands of the band, he's in trouble. "I can't live without being on the road," he says. ". . . I either turn into an alcoholic or a junkie 'cause I've got nothing else to do."

NEVER-ENDING STORY: DAVID CROSBY'S ARREST RECORD

1971
Arrested on pot charges.

1977
After performing for Jimmy Carter at the White House, Crosby, Stills and Nash are left alone in the Oval Office. So they spark up a joint.

1982
Crosby crashes his car en route to a demonstration at a nuclear power plant. When the ambulance crew pull him out they find Quaaludes, cocaine, and an unlicensed handgun. Two weeks later, he is arrested for possession of cocaine and another handgun.

1984
Crosby arrested again in possession of a dagger, heroin, cocaine, pot, and codeine.

1985
Crosby serves nine months of a five-year sentence in Texas.

1994
Crosby receives a liver transplant after his own nearly stopped functioning due to extensive alcohol and drug abuse.

2004
A month after telling a newspaper he'd not been tempted by drugs for years, Crosby is arrested by the NYPD after leaving an ounce of marijuana, a handgun, and a knife at a hotel in Manhattan.

The smell of opium is the least stupid smell in the world.
Pablo Picasso

> **When you smoke herb, herb reveal yourself to you. All the wickedness you do, the herb reveal it to your conscience, because herb make you meditate. It's a natural ting and it grows like a tree.**
> Bob Marley

AND FOR DESSERT? LSD

During a 1971 interview with *Rolling Stone* magazine, John Lennon was asked how the Beatles were introduced to LSD. He said: "A dentist in London laid it on George, me and the wives, without telling us, at a dinner party at his house. He was a friend of George's and our dentist at the time, and he just put it in our coffee or something."

Well, that's part of the story. The full story is, during the filming of *Help!*, the dentist friend of John and George's (rumored to be "Doctor Robert," from the *Revolver* album) had a dinner party where the conversation circled around the topic of LSD-guru Timothy Leary, a person Lennon had barely heard of. LSD was consumed, but no one seemed to feel any effect. At least, that's what John and George thought as they drove around Weybridge and central London at 10 miles an hour in the latter's Mini, with the wives in the back thinking they were now, officially, insane. Later, Lennon began drawing and imagined Harrison's house as a big submarine where they all lived. It's a shame that idea never came to anything . . .

> **Let me be clear about this: I don't have a drug problem, I have a police problem.**
> Keith Richards

AEROSMITH

According to Jerry Garcia, legendary stoner from legendary stoners' band the Grateful Dead, Aerosmith were the druggiest band he ever saw. That is some serious recommendation. Aerosmith were, without doubt, the originators of the all-American messed-up drug band. They were, famously, the first band to own mansions they'd never even seen, and by the mid-1970s, singer Steve Tyler and guitarist Joe Perry's insatiable appetite for intoxicants saw them renamed the Toxic Twins.

"Incredible excess," Tyler told *Blender* in 2002. "A swimming pool filled to the top with blow [cocaine] would be about right," he said, neglecting to mention his own love of heroin, Valium, marijuana, booze, and even muscle relaxants. ("I'd be so stoned . . . my eyes would cross, and I couldn't uncross them. I even remember driving like that.") Perry, meanwhile, used to nurse a love of heroin so all-enveloping he almost missed his own wedding day, he was so stoned. The group went sober in 1989 and have gone on to be one of the world's most successful stadium acts.

HOW TO DO DRUGS BADLY: DAVID CROSBY

David Crosby, guitarist and songwriter with the Byrds and Crosby, Stills, Nash, and Young, reckons he has made in excess of $25 million during his 40-plus years in music. Most of it went up in smoke, down his throat, or up his nose. Fired from the Byrds for his rampant egotism, Crosby formed the incredibly successful CSN(&Y) in 1968—a band he had originally planned to call the Frozen Noses in tribute to their cocaine habits. He recorded a solo album called *I Wish I Could Remember My Name* in 1971, but developed a love for freebasing (the stupidly dangerous precursor to crack) so powerful, he actually became accustomed to setting himself on fire with the propane torch necessary for smoking the coke. Later, he learned to drive with his knees so he could smoke crack in the car. In the 1980s, things got so bad he couldn't pay his mortgage and lived in a friend's house, even wearing his host's old clothes. Now sober, Crosby continues to tour—on and off—with Stephen Stills and Graham Nash.

Rolling in the aisles

the aisles

AN ABSENTMINDED STUMBLE THROUGH
THE DARKENED FLEA PIT
OF ROCK 'N' ROLL CINEMA

SHOULD ROCK STARS BE ALLOWED TO ACT?

Most attempts at the rock star/actor crossover are patchy at best (just check the Elvis stats: 31 films, 31 stinkers). Mick Jagger covered himself in glory in *Performance*, but then lost the plot in *Ned Kelly*, and pulled an even more risible performance out of the bag for 1992's stinker *Freejack*. Rapper Ice-T donned a kangaroo outfit for the appalling *Tank Girl* movie, but redeemed himself with an appearance in Ron Jeremy's 1996 comedy *Frankenpenis*, and has since built a solid post-rap career as a B-movie stalwart. Madonna? She started off well in *Desperately Seeking Susan*, but weigh that against *Shanghai Surprise*, *Dick Tracy*, and *Body of Evidence* . . .

On the other hand, David Bowie managed a half-successful movie career (top marks for 1976's *The Man Who Fell to Earth*), Mark Wahlberg is a better actor than he was a pop star (especially in *Boogie Nights*, and the 2001 rock movie *Rock Star*), and Bjork won plaudits for her work in Lars Von Trier's *Dancer in the Dark* (2000). Gavin Rossdale, the chisel-jawed looker who fronts rock group Bush, is currently having a go. Whether he turns out to be a Damon Albarn (embarrassing in the 1997 gangster flick *Face*) or a David Bowie remains to be seen.

FILMS PRODUCED BY GEORGE HARRISON

Little Malcolm (1974) · *The Life of Brian* (1979)
Black and Blue (1980) · *The Long Good Friday* (1980)
Time Bandits (1981) · *Privates on Parade* (1982)
The Missionary (1982) · *Scrubbers* (1983)
Bullshot (1983) · *A Private Function* (1984)
Water (1985) · *Mona Lisa* (1986)
Shanghai Surprise (1986) · *Withnail and I* (1987)
The Lonely Passion of Judith Hearne (1987)
Track 29 (1988) · *The Raggedy Rawney* (1988)
How to Get Ahead in Advertising (1989)
Checking Out (1989) · *Cold Dog Soup* (1990)
Nuns on the Run (1990)

BILBO MCCARTNEY?

At one point in 1968, a news story broke that the Beatles had secured the film rights for the J. R. R. Tolkien novel *The Lord of the Rings*, and that this was going to be their third live-action film. Although Ringo scotched the story in the *Daily Mirror* in June 1969, there were rumors flying around that John wanted to play Gollum and Ringo was going to be Gamgee. This was just one of several projects that were talked about but never happened, like the Joe Orton script *Up Against It*, which portrayed the boys as four aspects of one split personality and featured a gay subtext. Then there was the idea that the Fab Four were to play the *Four Musketeers* with Richard Lester directing them (eventually, Lester made the movie with Richard Chamberlain, Oliver Reed, Michael York, and Frank Finlay).

In the end, there are just the four official Beatles movies, and one of those (*Let It Be*, the 1970 document of the Beatles trying to make an album while splitting up) remains mysteriously difficult to get hold of. Still, the pleasures of *A Hard Day's Night* and *Help!* are manifold, the TV special *Magical Mystery Tour* is emerging as a psychedelic classic, and *Yellow Submarine* represents a high-water mark of British animation and pop imagery.

ALIEN BOWIE

The Man Who Fell to Earth (1976) is Bowie at his alien best, with a performance pulled out of him (he was at his drug-addled paranoid height during the filming) by director Nic Roeg. Many observers dismissed Bowie's portrayal as an alien (building a business empire on Earth in order to fund the saving of his drought-plagued home planet) as merely the star playing himself, but this misses the musician's understated skill (particularly in the scene where he pretends he can't sing). Bowie went on in the film biz with varying degrees of success—*Just a Gigolo*, *The Hunger*, *Merry Christmas, Mr. Lawrence*, *Absolute Beginners*, *The Last Temptation of Christ* (as Pontius Pilate, no less), and *Basquiat*, in which he played Andy Warhol. But nothing he's been in has come close to *The Man Who Fell to Earth*. This film is not only one of the best films ever made with a pop star in it, it's one of the best films ever made, period.

gods of rock

ROCK BIOPIC MUST-SEES

The Buddy Holly Story (1978)
Just one example of an actor looking more like the pop star he's pretending to be than the pop star did himself.

Superstar: The Karen Carpenter Story (1987)
Maybe the strangest and most artful low-budget biopic ever, this 43-minute animation uses Barbie dolls to tell Karen's tragic story. The filmmaker was sued by both Richard Carpenter and Mattel (the makers of Barbie), and the film is now officially unavailable.

The Doors (1991)
Val Kilmer plays Jim Morrison so convincingly, the real Jim Morrison starts to look like an imposter.

Backbeat (1994)
Damn good, this one.

Almost Famous (2000)
For obvious reasons, we fully support biopics of music journalists.

The Linda McCartney Story (2000)
A true jewel of the low-budget biopic.

In His Life: The John Lennon Story (2000)
Beatles biopics always have to be watched.

The Beach Boys: An American Family (2000)
Widely considered a propaganda piece aimed at resurrecting Mike Love's reputation.

24-Hour Party People (2002)
Imaginatively told story of Manchester's Factory Records, with Steve Coogan as Tony H. Wilson.

Man, your family is just too straight!
Charles Manson (Erik Passoja) to Dennis Wilson (Nick Stabile)
in *The Beach Boys: An American Family*

MUSICIANS PERFORMING AS THEMSELVES IN FICTION FILMS

The following have actually played a song (or part thereof):

Cheap Trick – *Daddy Day Care* (2003)

Brian Setzer (of the Stray Cats) – *The Country Bears* (2002)

Hanson – *Frank McKluskey CI* (2002)

Everclear – *Loser* (2000)

Bryan Adams – *House of Fools* (2000)

Ozomatli – *Never Been Kissed* (1999)

AC/DC – *Private Parts* (1997)

Mudhoney – *Black Sheep* (1996)

The Ramones – *Car 54, Where Are You?* (1994)

Aerosmith – *Wayne's World 2* (1993)

Joe Strummer – *I Hired a Contract Killer* (1990)

Jeff Beck – *Twins* (just counts—he's a member
of a nameless bar band in one scene) (1988)

Nick Cave & the Bad Seeds – *Wings of Desire* (1987)

Crime and the City Solution – *Wings of Desire* (1987)

Frankie Goes to Hollywood – *Body Double* (1984)

Bauhaus – *The Hunger* (Pete Murphy sings) (1983)

David Bowie – *Christiane F.* (1981)

The Yardbirds (the Jimmy Page lineup!) – *Blow-Up* (1966)

**We loathed the script because it was somebody trying to
write like we were in real life. In retrospect, Alun Owen
didn't do a bad job, but at the time we were self-conscious
about the dialogue. It felt unreal.**
John Lennon talking in 1970 about *A Hard Day's Night*

---

gods of rock

A MOCKUMENTARY, IF YOU WILL

"Hello, I'm Marti DeBergi . . ." says Rob Reiner at the beginning of *This Is Spinal Tap*, introducing the film he directs and appears in (as the director of the documentary) about a hapless British rock band's disastrous US tour. It was confusing enough in the pre-post-modern humor world of 1984 that many viewers (even members of rock bands) thought the band was for real. Iron Maiden thought it was about them and walked out of the screening, taking the whole thing as a personal insult. Brit boogie band Foghat claimed that their tour bus must have been bugged by the movie's makers, as a band member's girlfriend did attempt to run the group using astrology. Black Sabbath, meanwhile, had a design company build them a Stonehenge set so vast (three times the size of the actual Stonehenge, unlike Spinal Tap's, which was in danger of being crushed by the band's dwarf dancers) that it didn't fit through the doors of any of the venues they played. It has since become international law that any band walking from their dressing room to the stage with their guitars around their necks should at some point shout: "Hello, Cleveland!"

SLADE IN FLAME — AN OVERLOOKED CLASSIC

Slade's 1974 cash-in movie, *Flame*, is a *real* film, with a plot and everything, and probably the darkest pop movie ever made (literally—the budget didn't appear to stretch to much in the way of lighting). Noddy Holder was eager to show the unpleasant realities of the entertainment world the band had come from, and *Flame* depicts one band's rise from playing workingmen's clubs and wedding receptions in the 1960s, when rock 'n' roll was managed by thugs and gangsters, to the heights of mass success, as manipulated by equally ruthless corporate businessmen. The final irony is that once the movie came out, Slade's career went into free fall. Director Richard Loncraine went on to make 1982's *The Missionary* (with Michael Palin) and 2004's Brit-flick tennis romance screwup, *Wimbledon*. Noddy Holder went on to endorse a brand of salted snacks called Nobby's Nuts in a series of amusing television commercials.

FILMS WITH ROCK 'N' ROLL PLOTS

Expresso Bongo (1958)
Yes, the Cliff Richard vehicle, loosely based on Tommy Steele's story and full of seamy music biz cynicism.

That'll Be the Day (1972)
Ringo Starr, Keith Moon, and even the Bonzo Dog Doo-Dah Band's Vivian Stanshall make appearances.

Stardust (1974)
Dave Edmunds pops up in this one.

Rock 'n' Roll High School (1979)
The Ramones help a load of kids take over their high school following a teacher-organized record burning.

Airheads (1994)
Idiot band takes over radio station with fake guns in order to get airplay, starring Steve Buscemi, Brendan Fraser, Adam Sandler, and Michael McKean, who was David St. Hubbins in *This Is Spinal Tap*.

That Thing You Do! (1996)
One-hit wonders the Wonders ride their one hit for all it's worth in 1964, written and directed by Tom Hanks. The hit was written for the movie by Adam Schlessinger of ace US power pop rockers Fountains of Wayne.

Bandwagon (1996)
Fictional band Circus Monkey want to be pop stars, and realize what the music biz is *really* all about.

Velvet Goldmine (1998)
A load of Brit actors like Ewan McGregor get to pretend to be 1970s pop stars.

School of Rock (2003)
Jack Black plays Dewey Finn, who has been kicked out of his band and teaches 10-year-olds how to rock, with Led Zeppelin, AC/DC, and Black Sabbath as the teaching aids.

Oh, I fancy him, old rubber lips. He's had three number ones, two number twos and a number four.

The peculiar child girl/boy in *Performance*, eating beans and talking to Chas (James Fox) about Turner (Mick Jagger) as he takes a bath

gods of rock

THE ACTING BEATLE

By moping down by the canal in a rare moment of reflection and respite in the frenetic *Hard Day's Night*, Ringo made a name for himself as the acting Beatle. He was rewarded with the lead role in *Help!* and on the soundtrack album he sang the vaguely prophetic "Act Naturally" ("They're going to make a big star out of me . . ."). Of course, Ringo's non-Beatle efforts on the silver screen never came close to matching his Beatle fame. His first non-Beatle movie was 1968's *Candy*. Filming took 10 days out of his schedule and largely involved the filming of a sex scene with Ewa Aulin, a Swedish beauty who later appeared naked in a Monty Python sketch called "Full Frontal Nudity." *The Magic Christian*, in 1969, has Ringo as the lead, although it was essentially a Peter Sellers film. Ringo's modest assertion that he was being "used for the name" was an accurate reading of the situation. In 1971, he joined the cast of Frank Zappa's *200 Motels*, as Frank Zappa. He then played the brother of a blind gunslinger in the 1971 spaghetti western *Blindman* before tackling his most acclaimed role, in the rock 'n' roll movie *That'll Be the Day*.

Parts in wacky romps kept Ringo occupied in between solo albums and drinking through the rest of the 1970s (*Son of Dracula*, *Lisztomania*, *Sextette*), but 1981's Stone Age comedy *Caveman* was perhaps a goofy comedy too far and the acting jobs dried up, until he found his forte providing the voice-over for the animated TV series of *Thomas the Tank Engine*.

THE PRE-FAB FOUR

The great unsung predecessor of *This Is Spinal Tap*, and a fine example of British myth-puncturing, is the dizzying parody of the Beatles' career, *All You Need Is Cash*. Starring Monty Python's Eric Idle and the former Bonzo Dog Doo-Dah Band songwriting genius (and friend of the Beatles) Neil Innes, it features cameos from George Harrison, Mick Jagger, Ron Wood, and Paul Simon. Like Spinal Tap, the Rutles took on a life of their own, separate from the movie. In 1996, they released *Archaeology*, their answer to the Beatles' *Anthology* series, but in 2005, after nearly 30 years of sporadic recording and gigging, Neil Innes announced the last ever public performance of the Rutles.

The music biz plot line is a potential death trap for movie producers, but it doesn't stop them from trying. Here are some of the best (and worst):

Wild in the Streets (1968) stars Christopher Jones (hailed at the time as "the new James Dean") as a drug-pushing millionaire teen rock star who becomes president of the USA via the natty policy of shipping over-30s to concentration camps and dosing them up on LSD. Now *that's* a plot for a rock 'n' roll movie.

That'll Be the Day (1972), and its follow-up, *Stardust*, which has David Essex romping about with naked groupies and off his choppers on drugs.

Slade's *Flame* (1974) is the best show in this genre.

Breaking Glass (1980) has punk-lite 1980s glam scary robot-dancing Hazel O'Connor attempting to portray a genuinely tortured punk artist, and failing.

Prince's semi-autobiographical (which nearly makes it a biopic) *Purple Rain* (1984).

Spice World (1997) Rotten and cynical attempt at emulating a wacky Beatles-esque celluloid moment.

Eminem's screen debut in *8-Mile* (2002).

Be Cool (2005) Elmore Leonard potboiler novel, filmed largely just to have John Travolta and Uma Thurman dance together again.

> **In the midst of all this public bickering, "Let It Rot" was released as a film, an album, and a lawsuit. In 1970, Dirk sued Stig, Nasty, and Barry; Barry sued Dirk, Nasty, and Stig; Nasty sued Barry, Dirk, and Stig; and Stig sued himself accidentally. It was the beginning of a golden era for lawyers, but for the Rutles, live on a London rooftop, it was the beginning of the end.**
> The narrator of the Rutles documentary, *All You Need Is Cash*

EGO TRIPS

Rock movies not mentioned elsewhere, but included in case you thought we forgot them—we didn't.

Catch Us If You Can (1965)
The Dave Clarke Five run around a lot trying to be like the Beatles.

Sympathy for the Devil (1968)
Goddard's documentary of the Rolling Stones and pals working on the song of the same name in the studio, intercut with political rants and graffiti-spraying fun.

Head (1968)
A band created by television execs becomes real and gets Jack Nicholson to direct their movie.

Tommy (1975)
Overblown rock opera from the fevered imaginations of Pete Townshend and director Ken Russell with bad singing from Oliver Reed.

The Song Remains the Same (1976)
Led Zeppelin's monster egos running as wild and rampant as Robert Plant's symbolic stallion.

ABBA: The Movie (1977)
Music journalist chases ABBA around Australia trying to get an interview.

KISS Meets the Phantom of the Park (1978)
Cartoon rock band in cartoon strip horror movie.

Quadrophenia (1979)
Who-financed mod-revival movie.

The Music Machine (1979)
Brit attempt to cash in on the disco fever induced by the far, far superior *Saturday Night Fever*.

The Great Rock 'n' Roll Swindle (1980) Malcom McLaren's revisionist telling of the story of the Sex Pistols.

Rude Boy (1980)
The Clash make a film.

Give My Regards to Broadstreet (1984) McCartney vanity movie.

Rattle and Hum (1988)
U2 pretend they're American.

Depeche Mode: 101 (1989)
D. A. Pennebaker concert film that showed amazed Brits just how big DM had become in the USA.

Sexual icons

SEX SIRENS AND SEX MACHINES

MADONNA

The First Lady of Sex

Very few people who've ever lived have—metaphorical—balls as big as the artist born Madonna Louise Ciccone, on August 16, 1958, in Bay City, Michigan. Who else would have had the wit and pride to launch themselves globally with a track called "Like a Virgin," or allowed their fearlessness (and their ego) drive them to the point where, at the height of their fame, they released a book full of images of their own sexual fantasies, then bound the book in metal and attached a copy of a single called—hurrah!—"Erotic" encased in what appeared to be an oversized condom wrapper? No one, that's who.

Madonna became, and has stayed, one of the late 20th century's most iconic and influential figures by working the Catholic-friendly virgin/whore image to previously unimaginable heights across every conceivable medium. There have been clanging failures along the way—*Dick Tracy* or *Swept Away*, anyone?—but you don't stay as big a star as Madonna has for more than 20 years (and that's $448 million worth of capital big) by not being relentlessly, overpoweringly sexy.

10 RESOLUTELY NONSEXY BANDS WITH *SEX* IN THEIR NAMES

The Sex: Horrible 1990s rock band who were too awful to live.
Dub Sex: Horrible 1980s art/rock/dance outfit from England.
Sexx: Horrible 1990s rock band. Not sexxy at all.
Alien Sex Fiend: Horrible 1980s goth-horror group.
Carter the Unstoppable Sex Machine: Pig-ugly 1990s indie twats.
Sex Gang Children: Return of the horrible 1980s goth band.
Miranda Sex Garden: Horrible 1990s faux-classical troupe.
Disco Tex and the Sex-O-Lettes: Disco Tex died a virgin.
Cex: Clever, but not clever enough to avoid being trash.
Sex Pistols: Never heard of this lot, probably trash.

JIM MORRISON — HOW TO BLOW IT: REVEALED

Jim Morrison, pampered son of an admiral and lead singer of LA psyche-pop godheads the Doors, will, for a lot of people, remain forever young, forever utterly sexy. His Christ-like stare, razor-sharp cheekbones, and lean, fatless torso—captured in 1967, just four years before his death—that appear on the band's hugely successful *Best Of* speak to successive generations of adolescents (and it is adolescents; the band's appeal rarely lasts past people's early 20s) for whom the myth of sex and drugs and rock 'n' roll is still new, still exciting, still full of possibilities. For Morrison, however, the myth, taken to fully before he even joined the band, meant massive quantities of hallucinogens, riotous sexual abandon, and enough alcohol to bloat, stupefy, and, ultimately, kill a man in less than a decade. For a while, however, he still looked near perfect.

Morrison's favorite quote was from William Blake: "The road of excess leads to the palace of wisdom"; but for Morrison, that road led away from the palace of wisdom and toward a bathtub in a Parisian apartment where he died from a booze- and drug-assisted heart attack. Shame.

MICK JAGGER

At the age of 21, in late 1963, Mick Jagger was sexy in a way that no one had ever really been before. Lots of people had been handsome, sure, but no one had been so ugly-handsome that it actually felt a bit threatening, a bit intimidating. Put simply, Jagger was the archetypal rock singer. Full lips, long, thick hair, a waist the size of most people's wrists—Jagger was so stridently sexy he either turned you on or terrified the hell out of you. For many, it was the former and, consequently, even the more discerning women began to fall like overstimulated dominoes. From Chrissie Shrimpton, Marianne Faithfull, and Anita Pallenberg (his bandmate Keith's squeeze), through Marsha Hunt, Bianca de Macias, and Jerry Hall, right up to Brazilian model Luciana Gimenez and Sophie Dahl—the list is still growing, despite Jagger being well into his 60s. A sexual icon, no less. Not bad for a bloke from Dartford.

SEXY ROCK TRACKS

Serge Gainsbourg and Jane Birkin – "Je T'aime (Moi non Plus)"
"Apparently," the tittle-tattle went in 1969, "they're actually having sex!
Those Frenchies, eh!"

Barry White – "It's Ecstasy When You Lie Next to Me"
Best title of all time and a killer tune, too.

AC/DC – "You Shook Me All Night Long"
For *shook*, read: "did me like a blue-balled wildebeest."

Rolling Stones – "Rocks Off"
Filthy sounding in all the right ways and a beacon of light for Primal Scream.

Al Green – "Love and Happiness"
The original title was: "Banging like an outhouse door in the wind.
And happiness."

The Kinks – "You Really Got Me"
British pop finally understands what goes on between the belt
buckle and Beatle boot.

My Bloody Valentine – "Loveless"
An entire album of blissed-out, post-ecstasy sex rock made by an
otherwise incredibly unattractive band. Hurrah!

Marvin Gaye – "Let's Get It On"
Mr. Gaye liked to get straight to the point.

The Troggs – "Wild Thing"
If someone you know makes "everything groovy" then snap them up fast.

James Brown – "Hot Pants
(She Got to Use What She Got to Get What She Wants)"
The neatly hidden subtext being that a powerful woman can sometimes be
justified in (sniiip . . .)

My hose is my own. No Coke bottle, nothing stuffed down there.

Freddie Mercury

LEAST SEXY ROCK STARS

Michael Jackson: Enough said.

Meatloaf: Imagine the sweating.

Axl Rose: Whining ginger maggot. In a kilt.

Justin Hawkins (the Darkness): That hair. Those teeth.

Freddie Mercury: Those teeth. That hair!

Courtney Love: Please, put everything away.

Bill Wyman: Two words: Mandy Smith. One number: 13.

Gary Glitter: Likewise. Only worse.

Brian Wilson: Great songwriter, bad date.

Bono: Just tries too hard.

Eminem: Who could get past the bad mummy hang-up?

Sting: Self-love precludes you all. Forever.

Mick Hucknall: Never forget the shiny plastic jumpsuit.

Stuart Cable: Astonishingly, too ugly even for the Stereophonics.

BOB DYLAN

Okay, so the hoody-wearing old guy nearing his 70s (the one who got that awful disease you need to live in a cave with bats to catch) might not be the ladies' first choice. But 40 years ago it was a different story. In the mid-1960s, Bob Dylan had the highest hair, the sharpest mind, and the cruelest tongue—and which one of those could anyone resist? Listen to the *Live at the Carnegie Hall* CD and you can actually hear his guest and fellow-folkie Joan Baez (and most of the other women in the room) crumble, breathlessly, under his gaze. In the mid-1970s, after years of isolation, Dylan, now rocking the tousle-haired Jewish cowboy look, headed out on the Rolling Thunder Revue and was pursued everywhere he went by streams of groupies. Ultimately, Dylan proved that there was more to sex than just the sexual, and that old adage, *Sometimes your most important sexual organ is your brain*, remains as true as ever.

ELVIS — THE HAIR, THE LIPS, THE SNARL, THE HIPS

The product of a deeply sullen father and a mother he could never hope to love enough, Elvis was raw, poor, and almost overpoweringly shy, but his voice and his (early) purity had an enormous, immediate effect. Elvis's sexuality was so near the surface it was dangerous, and so he was attacked from all sides. His records were seized upon and destroyed by the thousands; towns banned all Elvis-related tours and shows. TV networks reared up against this defiant music until they realized there was money to be made. And the money would be made because this young man looked *really* good in tight trousers and he sang okay, too. Elvis was the first post-war sexual icon. The floodgates were, officially, open.

DAVID BOWIE

If Mick Jagger was sexy in a way that no one had been before, then David Bowie was sexy in a way that no one has been since. The classic art-school over-achiever, Bowie showed first Britain, and then the rest of the world, that theatricality, bisexuality, and cross-dressing all had their place in the rock pantheon. Here was a character who was so weird even his eyes didn't match, a character so sexually ambiguous and alluring that generations have seemingly forgotten about, or forgiven, Bowie's love of the bright orange hairdo.

As Ziggy Stardust, a name now completely hollowed out and made ludicrous by time, Bowie became a debauched, alien sex fiend, an amoral princeling touring the world fueled only by cocaine and fellatio. When he announced he was bisexual (a claim Bowie has long since retracted) the press went wild, fully aware that homosexuality was still, technically, illegal. Now, as he approaches 60, Bowie has matured into an immaculately dressed rock statesman, married, predictably, to the equally immaculate Iman. He, without a doubt, still has it.

> **I'm pro-heterosexual. I can't get enough of women.**
> **I have sex as often as possible . . .**
> Axl Rose (Guns N' Roses)

HUGELY UNLIKELY SEX SYMBOLS

Barry White
A big ball of sweat-streaked sexual ecstasy

Shane McGowan
Last of the doomed romantics

Kurt Cobain
Cry-baby self-harmer—nice eyes, though

Nick Rhodes
An incredibly boring man with bleached hair

Lemmy
Warts + booze + amphetamines + fag-breath = sex

Sid Vicious
Scabrous junkie idiot – nice hair, though

Britney Spears
All downhill after the schoolgirl look

50 Cent
Mouth-breathing bullet-wastebasket—nice tits, though

Keith Richards
Still your classic terrible, ruined beauty

Ringo Starr
What does that big nose signify?

Morrissey
The world's first sexless sex symbol

Janis Joplin
Like Lemmy, only worse

Be strong, believe in freedom and in God, love yourself, understand your sexuality, have a sense of humor, masturbate.
Madonna

DEBBIE HARRY

The perfect mix of art and commerce, of street style and high fashion, of punk and pop, of now and of always, Debbie Harry was already a seriously sexy woman of 32 (ancient by pop's Lolita-like standards) by the time she hit mainstream consciousness in the summer of 1977. Here was a woman who had served time as a bunny girl, taken masses of drugs with the Velvet Underground, a woman whose band, Blondie, were the first to play regularly at New York's legendary CBGB, before Television, the Ramones, or Talking Heads got, so to speak, a sniff. When Blondie broke internationally she became New York's brightest star, sought out by Andy Warhol, Truman Capote, and William Burroughs. Reinventing the raw sensuality of Marilyn Monroe years ahead of Madonna, Courtney Love, and Gwen Stefani, Harry was pure sex; all the collected, starlet allure of the 1940s, 1950s, 1960s, and 1970s resided in her, kept safe by the best bottle-blonde job anyone's ever seen.

ROBERT PLANT

Shirt cut to the waist, washed-out denim jeans barely containing the no doubt considerable beast within, chest-rug suitably sprinkled with diamond-drips of sweat, Robert Plant was, in his Led Zeppelin heyday, the rock singer that all other rock singers wish they were. While his band may have been built on serious muso-dom, it was Plant's fevered wail that made sure it wasn't just chin-stroking, beer-chugging dudes clogging up the front rows of Zeppelin's arena shows in the 1970s.

Probably the only person ever to have been born in Wolverhampton and, some years later, go on to exclaim to a reporter that they're "a golden god," Plant lived the dream at a time when none of it seemed stupid yet. The band traveled in a private jet—*The Starship*—rented out whole floors of hotels, and became so legendary for their sexual excess, including the infamous incident where a ginger-haired fan was abused with a fish ("A red snapper for your red snapper . . ."), that an entire industry emerged from former Led Zeppelin employees writing books about their eye-popping escapades. None of which would have happened without Plant.

BANNED: TOO SEXY FOR RADIO 1

Cliff Richard – "Honky Tonk Angel"
Prodigy – "Smack My Bitch Up"
Serge Gainsbourg and Jane Birkin – "Je T'aime (Moi non Plus)"
Pete Shelley – "Homosapien"
Scott Walker – "Jackie"
The Troggs – "I Can't Control Myself"
The Au Pairs – "Come Again"
The Rolling Stones – "Let's Spend the Night Together"
Frankie Goes to Hollywood – "Relax"
George Michael – "I Want Your Sex" (post-watershed play only)

PRINCE

Playing the guitar has gone from being the sexiest thing in the world to, roughly, being on a par with directing traffic in about 20 years—a tragedy for Prince Rogers Nelson, who, in his prime, had the world's largest collection of oddly phallic guitars that now just look ridiculous. Prince himself, however, still looks great, perhaps not as great as he did in the thong and flasher's coat on the cover of 1980's *Dirty Mind* LP (themes: oral sex, threesomes, incest), but that's not a look you can carry off forever. Prince's appeal has always been rooted in the way he is as much female as male, as much black as white. His attraction lies in the confidence he has in his own genius as much as it does in his minuscule waist and high cheekbones. Someone who has the wit—and balls—to feature a huge flying bed as the centerpiece of their live show (as Prince did in the late 1980s) is clearly something very special indeed.

It has always taken more than visual input to make me want to join a man [sexually]. I do recognize beauty, but I think a redwood tree is beautiful and it doesn't make me want to straddle a branch.
Grace Slick (Jefferson Airplane)

ROBBIE WILLIAMS

Famously labeled "a fat dancer from Stoke" by ex-mate Noel Gallagher, Robbie Williams actually poses the only threat to Noel's brother Liam's claim to be the sexiest rock star of the 1990s. Despite a seemingly inescapable urge to turn every gaze into a smirk, every grin into a grimace, Robert Peter Williams remains the man most likely to, well, do almost anything to anyone at any time. While his career may have stalled in America and his "private life" (a misnomer if ever there was one) is proving equally disappointing, Williams has grown from the dirty-looking one in Take That to the pooped-looking one post–Take That, to a cleaned-up, gently crinkled Tom Jones figure, someone whose charisma and sex appeal have long since become so ingrained in our consciousness that we forget how *Vogue*, a magazine not known for their liking of male cover stars, put Williams upfront alongside Brazilian sexpot Gisele Bundchen, or how women's magazine readers repeatedly vote him Sexiest Man Alive. He claims to have slept with four of the five Spice Girls, too. But we shouldn't hold that against him.

LIAM GALLAGHER

The yin to Robbie Williams's yang, the best rock 'n' roll singer Britain has ever produced, and the real reason Oasis have stayed—and will stay—one of live music's biggest attractions, Liam Gallagher is a star writ large. Here is a man with Bambi's eyes and Thumper's fists, a man who spent much of the 1990s sleeping his way around the world fueled by cocaine and alcohol, a man whose "love child" with Lisa Moorish (also the mother to Pete Doherty's child) came to light just a week after his wedding to Patsy Kensit. But being the world's favorite Bad Boy is a job Gallagher was unwilling to give up, and the stories of wholesale sexual excess continued right up to the divorce before he leapt straight into a relationship with former All Saint Nicole Appleton.

Gallagher has mellowed, but the echoes of that V-sign-flashing, fisherman's-hat-wearing, coke-snorting, lager-swilling sex monster remain hidden just behind those famously hooded eyes. Ladies, beware.

Sexual healing

WIVES, LOVERS, NIGHTMARES

10 RULES OF GOOD GROUPIE-DOM

1. No sleeping over.

2. No meeting in public except for dinner or drinks.

3. No calls before 9 PM.

4. No lovemaking — only sex.

5. The less eye contact the better.

6. No emotional discussions.

7. Calling out the wrong name during sex is okay.

8. No falling asleep after sex. Get up, get dressed, go home.

9. If anyone asks who you are, the response should
be: "_____'s cousin."

10. No "glove," no love.

COURTNEY LOVE

Courtney Love has come closest to encompassing the entire history of groupie/wife/crazydom than anyone before or since. She is an actress, songwriter, singer, guitarist, and mother, but she's most famous for marrying Kurt Cobain in 1992 and burying him in 1994 before going on to huge success of her own with Hole.

Love, the product of a deeply unhappy home, met Cobain in 1989. She became pregnant by him in 1992 and during her pregnancy *Vanity Fair* reported Love was still using heroin, a claim that saw her having to fight for her daughter's custody.

Thirteen years later, she was fighting for custody again after being caught with prescription drugs but no prescription. At a 2004 rehab attempt in Malibu, Love is said to have "danced naked for three hours" before staff could get her dressed. She threatens a new band. Called Bastard. Rumors are rife that she is pregnant with British comic Steve Coogan's baby.

SUZE "SUZE" ROTOLO

In early summer of 1961, Susan Rotolo, a highly educated, politically active teenage devotee of Byron and Brecht, attended a Monday night hootenanny at Gerde's in Greenwich Village. On stage that night was a 20-year-old Bob Dylan. One July night, after a daylong party at Riverside Church, the young folksinger began flirting. In mid-December 1961, Dylan moved into his first rented apartment, a tiny place above Bruno's Spaghetti Shop on West Fourth Street, and Suze moved in with him.

"We influenced each other," she has said. "But the guy saw things. He was definitely way, way ahead. His radar was flying."

In February 1963, right in the middle of a frozen-looking Fourth Street (though some Dylanologists claim it's actually Great Jones Street, one block south of Fourth), Bob and Suze, recently reunited after seven months' separation, had their love captured for ever by Don Hunstein, the staff photographer at Dylan's record label, Columbia. The picture ended up on the cover of *The Freewheelin' Bob Dylan* and Suze herself became an icon. When they split up, Dylan told her: "Never let anybody take up your space."

In the mid-1970s, Suze turned down Dylan's out-of-the-blue offer to see each other again for her husband's sake. She now says her decision was a violation of Dylan's advice.

> **We thought we could be stars. I loved being a groupie, I loved hanging out with bands. But I wanted groupies!**
> "Supergroupie" Pamela Des Barres

PENNY LANE

"I always tell the girls never take it seriously. If you never take it seriously then you never get hurt. If you never get hurt then you always have fun, and if you ever get lonely you can just go to the record store and visit your friends."
Penny Lane in *Almost Famous*

Cameron Crowe's *Almost Famous* is a semi-autobiographical account of his own experiences as a teenage rock journalist in the early 1970s. On his first, disastrous, attempt to interview Black Sabbath, he meets Penny Lane, not a groupie but a "Band-Aid," a girl who, in theory, develops long-term relationships with traveling musicians.

Played by Kate Hudson, Lane is at once wise and utterly naiive, someone who is taken up quickly and dropped even more speedily when the legitimate wives and girlfriends appear. Based on Crowe's real-life friend Pennie Trumble, who was known as "Pennie Lane," Hudson's portrayal is cinema's most sensitive, lucid treatment of groupie/Band-Aid-dom in existence.

PAMELA ANDERSON

Pamela Anderson is, at the time of this writing, about to marry Mötley Crüe drummer Tommy Lee for the third time. Now, we know, from their delightful home video, that Lee can steer a speedboat with his penis, so maybe we shouldn't be so surprised. Before their first marriage they'd only known each other for 96 hours, and during the marriage Anderson filed for divorce twice. In 2002, she revealed she had contracted the hepatitis C virus from Lee—apparently from sharing tattoo needles, a romantic way to get it, no doubt. What this third marriage will mean to some of Anderson's former special friends—Ben Affleck, Scott Baio, Dean Cain, John Cusack, Fred Durst, Kid Rock, Bret Michaels, and Sylvester Stallone—remains to be seen.

GTO: GIRLS TOGETHER "OUTRAGEOUSLY"

They were the world's first groupie supergroup.

They all had special names: Miss Pamela, Miss Christine, Miss Lucy, Miss Sandra, Miss Sparky, Miss Cynderella, and Miss Mercy.

Frank Zappa was their musical director.

Their one and only LP, *Permanent Damage* tanked on release but is now a superhip collectors' piece.

The group split up after a series of drug busts—Zappa was famously anti-drugs.

Miss Pamela became, briefly, the world's most famous groupie with her memoirs *I'm with the Band*.

Miss Sparky worked for a short time as an executive at Disney.

A documentary about Miss Mercy has been in development for some time.

No one's really sure if the *O* actually stood for "Outrageously" or something else . . .

LEE ANGEL

An ex-girlfriend (and "orgy partner") of Little Richard and Screamin' Jay Hawkins, Lee Angel—aka Angel Robinson or Robin Lee—was a burlesque performer who began her career on the East Coast in 1956 with her infamous "World of Mirth Show." Angel later became the one and only striptease artiste/dancer to headline early rock 'n' roll shows on the southern states' version of the UK's toilet circuit, the chitlin' circuit. Angel took her act all over the world before retiring from stripping in 1977. In the last few years, Little Richard has publicly stated that Angel has been his partner for more than 50 years.

YOKO ONO

A student of Fluxus, an ex-wife, a mother, and an established avant-garde ("I avant-garde a clue"—George Harrison) artist long before she met John Lennon, Yoko Ono has never lost the ability to rub people up the wrong way. Or get them thinking. New York's *Village Voice* claimed that Ono had invented the "downtown" art boom as early as 1960, and she was the first to rent a loft to present events and gigs such as those she organized with LaMonte Young. Ono always says that her work is constantly changing; she never likes anything to be final. For her, the idea that a piece of art has a finish makes her nervous. "My art is about the journey rather than the end product," she has said. Now in her 70s, her work still fills galleries across the world.

MYRA LEWIS

In October 1956, J. W. Brown, a musician and cousin of Jerry Lee Lewis's whom he had never met, passed through Jerry Lee's home town of Ferriday, Louisiana, to find the star broke, depressed, and out of work. Brown was on his way home to Memphis and, desperate to restart his career, Lewis begged him for a lift. On arriving at rock 'n' roll's most important town, he was welcomed into Brown's home by his wife, Lois, and their 12-year-old daughter, Myra Gale. At the time, Jerry Lee Lewis was 24 and had already been married twice.

Just over a year later, on December 12, 1957, and without Brown's or Lois's knowledge or approval, the pair were married in Mississippi. Soon after, Myra accompanied Lewis to the UK on tour, but when the newspapers discovered how young she was they went berserk. Then it was revealed that one of Lewis's previous marriages had not been legally terminated; the tour was pulled and the entire entourage returned to the States. Myra gave birth to a son, Steve Allen, in 1959, who died aged just five after accidentally drowning in the family swimming pool. The marriage survived until 1970.

NANCY SPUNGEN

Sid Vicious's murdered ex, Nancy Spungen, may have seemed like the world's most annoying, screeching junkie groupie. But she wasn't. She was mentally ill and had been, according to her mother's book, *I Don't Want to Live Like This*, since suffering brain damage during a traumatic birth. As a baby Nancy constantly screamed and yelled; she had terrible nightmares accompanied by delirium tremens and was diagnosed as schizophrenic. A heroin addict since 15, Spungen was the imperfect foil for ex-speed-dealer Vicious, and the pair moved to New York at the end of a disastrous Sex Pistols US tour in the autumn of 1978. On October 12 of that year, Nancy Spungen died on the bathroom floor of Room 100 of the Chelsea Hotel after suffering a single knife wound in the lower abdomen. She was 20.

THE HENDRIX EXPERIENCE

On the evening of September 17, 1970, Monika Dannemann went to pick up her boyfriend, guitarist Jimi Hendrix, from a party he had been to at a friend's London apartment. Monika claims Hendrix later showed her a selection of pills that had been given to him by people at the party, but insists he threw them out of the car window as she drove them back to their apartment. Hendrix insisted he had taken no drugs whatsoever at the party and, on arriving home around 3 AM, the pair sat and talked until 7 AM, when Dannemann fell asleep. On awakening at 11 AM, she noticed Hendrix had vomited in his sleep and tried to wake him. She couldn't. Dannemann says her boyfriend was still breathing. She also says she noticed empty sleeping pill containers on the floor. An ambulance arrived at 11:27 AM, and the crew told Dannemann that Hendrix was "in a deep sleep" and that he would be fine. They then took him to the hospital. When Hendrix entered St. Mary Abbot Hospital he was alive and breathing. At 12:45 PM, he was pronounced dead. Monika Dannemann did believe in the possibility that Hendrix was murdered. Tony Brown's book, *The Final Days of Jimi Hendrix*, suggests she may have been involved in Hendrix's death. Dannemann committed suicide in April 1996.

gods of rock

JEANINE ST. HUBBINS — WIFE OF SPINAL TAP SINGER

Jeanine on David

"He plays things to me, sometimes when he's worked up, and he's got a new bit he wants to tell me about. I say: 'Yeah, that's good,' or 'that's bad,' or 'that's shit,' or whatever, you know."

David on Jeanine
"She is brutally frank."

Derek Smalls (bass)
"Things went wrong more smoothly once Jeanine took over."

Jeanine on David
"The shock of blond, the blaze of red velvet, the aura of Remy Martin."

David on Jeanine
"Before I met Jeanine my life was cosmically in shambles. I was using bits and pieces of whatever Eastern philosophies happened to drift through my transom."

Derek on Jeanine
"Nigel never really wanted her on stage. He gave her a tambourine with no bells and no drum skin to play. A wooden ring!"

Jeanine on David (again)
"He is the dream warrior I have known in my slumbers for so many years."

Rock is really about dick and testosterone.

Courtney Love

PAULA YATES

The British Courtney Love? After shooting to fame presenting the TV rock show *The Tube*, Yates became one of the country's most famous women. She married "Saint" Bob Geldof shortly after the birth of their first daughter, Fifi, in 1986. During her marriage to Bob, Paula had an affair with Terence Trent D'Arby before moving on to INXS front man Michael Hutchence in 1995. A messy divorce and custody battle followed. In 1996, Paula and Michael had a daughter, Heavenly Hirrani Tiger Lily, and that same year, Paula was busted twice for drug possession. Michael and Paula were engaged to be married when he died in 1997 as a result of auto-erotic asphyxiation. Paula had a nervous breakdown and began dating a man she met in drug rehab. In 1998, she lost custody of her children. In 1999 she began a relationship with Michael Flatley. In 2000, Tiger Lily found her dead at home with heroin, cannabis, pills, and alcohol found strewn around her.

BEBE BUELL

Another contender for the title of real-life Penny Lane, Bebe Buell is a former model and *Playboy* centerfold who has famously been linked to Mick Jagger, Jimmy Page, Todd Rundgren, Steven Tyler, Elvis Costello (who, apparently, still places secret messages to her in his songs), and Stiv Bators.

Having deserted her modeling career to set up a home with Todd Rundgren, Buell says she would have affairs with rock stars partly to get back at her notorious, bed-hopping partner, but mostly because she really, really wanted to. So Mick Jagger is a "sweet, caring man." Jimmy Page, the Led Zeppelin guitarist famous for his strange kinks and taste for black magic gave her "the most wholesome sex imaginable." Keith Richards never had his turn, but Buell says she did enjoy peeping at his "huge erection."

Rundgren, of course, raised Buell's daughter Liv—conceived with Aerosmith singer Steven Tyler—as his own. Liv "fired" her overbearing mom a few years ago.

SUGGESTIONS FROM YOKO ONO'S *GRAPEFRUIT* (1964)

Painting to hammer a nail
Hammer a nail in the center of a piece of glass. Send each fragment to an arbitrary address.

Painting to exist only when it's copied or photographed
Let people copy or photograph your paintings. Destroy the originals.

Cloud piece
Imagine the clouds dripping. Dig a hole in your garden to put them in.

Travel piece
Make a key. Find a lock that fits. If you find it, burn the house that is attached to it.

Body piece
Stand in the evening light until you become transparent or until you fall asleep.

ANGIE BOWIE

In the summer of 1975, when David Bowie was in LA after the success of the sessions that produced the *Young Americans* album, his marriage to Angie was in serious trouble. He also had serious financial problems, and his cocaine habit was raging out of control. But Angie recalls another, more worrying activity, namely a deepening interest in the occult. While David consistently denied these interests, Angie, Marianne Faithfull, and Amanda Lear all published autobiographies that alluded to it. Angie says her husband was vulnerable to sycophants and hangers-on while he was addicted to cocaine. It has been alleged that Bowie scribbled kabbalistic calculations on his own correspondence, stored his own urine in a fridge, and, according to Faithfull, was obsessed with preventing anyone getting hold of his nail clippings. Angie points out this sort of voodoo superstition—where bodily waste could be put to evil uses—are found in some of Aleister Crowley's secret teachings.

Rock wackos

THE ONES WHO WEREN'T PRETENDING

MADNESS IN SONGS

"21st Century Schizoid Man" – King Crimson

"Bonkers in Phoenix" – Fall

"Crazy" – Seal

"Crazy Chick" – Charlotte Church

"Crazy Crazy Nights" – Kiss

"Crazy in Love" – Beyoncé

"Go Insane" – Lindsey Buckingham

"Insane" – Alice Donut

"Insane" – Texas

"Insane" – The Orb v. Meat Beat Manifesto

"Insane in the Brain" – Cypress Hill

"I Think I'm Paranoid" – Garbage

"Love Is Paranoid" – The Distillers

"Mental" – Eels

"Mr. Mental" – The Eighties Matchbox B-Line Disaster

"Paranoid" – Black Sabbath

"Paranoid" – Grand Funk Railroad

"Paranoid" – Megadeth

"Paranoid" – The Dickies

"Paranoid Android" – Radiohead

"Paranoid & Sunburnt" – Skunk Anansie

Psycho Girl - Busted

A lot of people think I'm clinically mad.
Morrissey

British rock 'n' roll was birthed in part in a messy apartment above a shop on London's Holloway Road. This was where Joe Meek, the creator of some of the biggest hit records of the age, lived and pioneered recording techniques that are still used today.

Meek was the UK's first independent record producer, and his apartment was home to an array of electronic bits and pieces, tape machines and wires with which he created the sound of the future. His biggest hit, the sci-fi-sounding "Telstar," was a massive international seller (it was the first ever record by a UK act to hit the US number 1 spot) and was recorded in his apartment. Mrs. Thatcher later claimed this to be her favorite record of all time.

Madness stalked this eccentric genius. He claimed to have made contact with Buddy Holly during a séance. He started setting up tape recorders in graveyards in an attempt to record the dead speaking. He became obsessed with the idea that the recording company Decca was stealing his ideas by placing hidden microphones in his wallpaper. Depression, paranoia, and drug use culminated in tragedy on February 3, 1967 (the eighth anniversary of Buddy Holly's death), when he murdered his landlady and then committed suicide with a rifle.

> **I want to be promoted as a madman whose influences come from trees, wind, earth, birds, fire and water, stamping my muddy boots all over EMI's well-tended carpets.**
> Lee "Scratch" Perry

MAD BAND NAMES

Insane Clown Posse – Detroit rap rockers, homeboy rivals of Eminem

Madness – The Nutty Boys

Mad Professor – Collaborator with Lee Perry and Massive Attack

Crazy Frog – Ringtone genius

Crazy Horse – Neil Young's backup band

Psycho Versatile

Psycho Kitten

Psycho Craig

OZZY OSBOURNE

Ah! Ozzy. The original madman of rock. The former singer of black country metal merchants Black Sabbath, Ozzy Osbourne's antics have kept rock fans amused for over three decades now, although his immense booze and drug intake have given him permanent shakes and the wide-eyed, perpetually surprised gaze of the recovering addict. Ozzy's behavior, carried out without any trace of malice, is the stuff of legend: He bit the head off a dove during a meeting with his new record company. The biting resulted in him being banned from the offices. He then bit the head off a bat that a fan threw onto the stage. It was an impulsive, Ozzy-esque moment that led to him having to suffer a series of immensely painful and disabling rabies shots.

One of his most spectacular stunts was when he was on tour in America. One night in Texas, his raging alcoholism was such that his wife, the also legendary Sharon, confiscated his clothes so he wouldn't be able to go out and get booze. Undaunted, Ozzy swiped one of Sharon's dresses and vamoosed. He got as drunk as a lord, and found himself needing to pee. He peed on a nearby wall, only to discover that it was the famed Alamo, virtually a holy shrine in Texas. He was arrested by an apoplectic state trooper and thrown into jail. His next album? *Diary of a Madman*, of course.

Michael Jackson never stood a chance, really. He was the 7th of 9 children and, with 10 other members of the family, grew up in a two-bedroom house as a Jehovah's Witness. He had a record deal as part of the Jackson 5 when he was 10, and was world famous shortly afterward. He was a multi-millionaire at 21, thanks to his debut solo album *Off the Wall* selling 7 million copies, and he made even more cash from *Thriller* (50 million copies sold and counting) a few years later in 1982. He has been famous for nearly 40 years. The first signs that all was not well came with Jackson's face—it was changing shape *and* color. Then there was Neverland, his enormous theme-park-cum-home in California, home to many llamas and, of course, Bubbles, the chimp. Bubbles would often be seen out and about with Jackson and was considered to be a close friend rather than a pet. Once, it was claimed that Jackson left a dinner he was hosting in order to shave Bubbles's bottom. The chimp slept in Jackson's bedroom, too. In 1994, Jackson married Lisa Marie Presley, the daughter of Elvis. The marriage ended two years later; Jackson married Deborah Jeanne Rowe, and the couple had two children. Their godparents are Macaulay Culkin and Elizabeth Taylor. Jackson and Rowe divorced in 1999, and in 2002 Jackson had another child, Michael Joseph Jackson III, aka Blanket. It was Blanket who got dangled out of a hotel window in Berlin while Martin Bashir was making a documentary about the star. And it was during this documentary that Jackson confirmed he slept with children. In his bed. And this after a spectacular court case in 1993 when he was accused of pedophilia and only narrowly avoided prison. Once again, in 2005, Jackson was found innocent of the same charges, but a further trial, together with the attempts to physically transform himself into Peter Pan, have left him, now approaching his 50s, deeply scarred.

Dogs smoke in France.
Ozzy Osbourne

gods of rock

> **It's the music that kept us all from going crazy. You should have two radios in case one gets broken.**
> Lou Reed

FRIGHTENING

There aren't too many genuinely psychotic or possibly psychopathic rock stars around. Many pretend, but nearly all are imposters, using the peculiar attraction around madness as a kind of pantomimic crutch for their careers. There are those, however, who are the real deal. El Duce, for example, was a Seattle resident and singer for the band the Mentors. He was partly responsible for the ubiquitous Parents Music Resource Center (PMRC) PARENTAL ADVISORY: EXPLICIT LYRICS stickers you see on CDs, when the lyrics for the Mentors' tune "Golden Showers" were read out in the congressional hearing that led to the introduction of the stickers.

Following the death of Kurt Cobain, El Duce claimed that he'd been offered $50,000 by Courtney Love to kill her husband. El Duce himself was killed when he was hit by a train in 1997.

More frightening than El Duce, however, was G. G. Allin. He fronted many bands in his time, including the Murder Junkies. He was named (by his mad father, who would sometimes dig graves in the dirt floor of the wood cabin the family lived in) Jesus Christ Allin. G. G. traveled around America, playing shows, living day to day, claiming himself to be the only true living spirit of rock 'n' roll.

On stage he would perform naked, wolfing down the piles of unidentified drugs audience members would hurl at him; he would urinate and defecate, and roll around in his own mess, and cut his body until he was covered in blood. He promised that he would commit suicide on stage on Hallowe'en, 1990, and that he would take some of the audience with him. In the end, he died of a heroin overdose after playing a show in New York in 1993.

Brian Wilson sang pretty songs with the band he formed with his brothers and cousin, the Beach Boys. With their matching striped shirts and feel-good tunes about surfing, they were massively popular, particularly in mainstream America.

Brian was the songwriter and was painfully shy, but as the band's career progressed, his real problems—and genius—emerged. The Beach Boys album *Pet Sounds* was a masterpiece, and inspired the Beatles to better it with *Sgt. Pepper's Lonely Hearts Club Band*. But Brian Wilson's success, drug intake, and mental instability got the better of him, and during the sessions for the *Pet Sounds* follow-up, *Smile*, Wilson was heavily into LSD and behaving erratically. In his home, he had a piano placed in a sandbox to recreate the feeling of being at the beach; in another room was a dope tent. While recording a song about fire (with everyone wearing fireman's helmets and with a fire raging in a fire bucket), a real fire broke out. Wilson was convinced that the recording session was responsible. The album was rejected by the rest of the Beach Boys as being too freaky, and the record company hated it, too.

Brian was shattered by the experience, by drugs, and by depression. He took to his bed, staying there for two years, grew a huge beard, and got very fat. He was looked after by Dr. Eugene Landy, a clinical psychologist believed to have been a negative influence. It took a court case to rid Brian of Landy, and years of traditional therapy before Wilson could start working again.

> **I think it's probably a good thing to be considered stable, but with a capacity for madness.**
>
> Wayne Coyne, the Flaming Lips

WHEN THE FAN IS EVEN MADDER

Bjork

In 1996, a man called Ricardo Lopez, obsessed with Bjork, sent her a package containing an acid bomb. According to some reports, he wanted to render Bjork ugly so they could get together in the afterlife. He then made a video of himself committing suicide.

Madonna

Homeless drifter Robert Dewey Hoskins was convinced that Madonna was his wife and threatened to kill her in 1995. He received 10 years in jail for his trouble.

Robbie Williams

Robbie gets hate mail and obsessive green-ink missives by the sackload, but in 2002, he fled his London home when he discovered two bullet holes in a window.

George Harrison

In 1999, the former Beatle was attacked in his home by a deranged stalker, Mike Abram. George tussled with the man and was stabbed. "He wasn't a burglar," said George, "but he certainly wasn't auditioning for the Traveling Wilburys." He was, though, a former heroin addict, who was declared criminally insane by a court and ordered to be detained indefinitely at a secure hospital.

John Lennon

In December 1980, Lennon was murdered outside the Dakota Building where he lived in New York by the delusional loner Mark Chapman. Chapman had already had stints in mental hospitals and was expected to plead insanity at his trial. Instead he pleaded guilty and was sentenced to life imprisonment. Three parole requests have been refused.

BABBLING

Lee Perry, the man who discovered Bob Marley and is responsible for the sound of Jamaican dub reggae, is, and pretty much always has been, an eccentric character bordering on the fruitcake. The walls of his studio, the legendary Black Ark, were covered in scrawls of tiny writing. There was a pond in the drum booth. Then one day he painstakingly crossed out every word of his tiny graffiti. He was seen walking around hitting the ground with a hammer and spouting nonsense. Then he burned his studio down. He has since said he did it because Bob Marley had recorded in there, and that he was evil. He said that people were stealing his music and the only way to stop the theft was to get rid of the studio. Around the same time (1979), he announced that he realized he was a white man. When he visited the UK in the 1980s, he told journalists that he was going to marry Margaret Thatcher, and that he was the king of England; he alarmed one writer when he started eating money. Lee Perry now lives in Switzerland.

JAZ HAS GONE TO ICELAND

Killing Joke were one of the most popular post-punk outfits to emerge in the late 1970s. Their densely packed and furious debut album was as bleak and frightening as the artwork that adorned it. No surprise, then, when it turned out that Killing Joke's front man, Jaz Coleman, had a tendency toward apocalyptic visions.

By 1982, Jaz had lost the plot entirely. Enraged by a bad review given by *Melody Maker*, he turned up at the offices of the music paper with a trash bag filled with rotting, maggot-infested liver and dumped it onto the receptionist's desk. Jaz then became convinced that the apocalypse was imminent and that the only place where it could be avoided was, mysteriously, Iceland, where the band relocated.

Eventually Jaz conceded that there was no apocalypse, and the band returned to the UK. Jaz is now a widely respected composer of classical music, and still writes and performs with Killing Joke.

Overindulgence in LSD has often been cited as the reason for the mental collapse of Syd Barrett, Pink Floyd's charismatic songwriter, but it's fairly obvious to most observers (and to the rest of the band) that Syd was ill in the first place, and that drugs only exacerbated his behavior.

This behavior is summed up by his notorious appearance on *The Pat Boone Show* in the USA. The band were supposed to mime, but Syd stared at the camera with his arms hanging limply by his side. When Pat Boone attempted an interview, Syd stared at him blankly. Roger Waters gallantly stepped in and answered the questions.

On another occasion, Syd crushed a load of tranquilizers into a tub of Brylcreem and dumped the mixture on his head before going on stage. Under the stage lights, the mixture melted and ran down his face, and Syd convinced himself his head was melting.

By 1968, Syd was no longer an active member of the band, and he became increasingly reclusive and erratic. There were two solo albums in 1970, *The Madcap Laughs* and *Barrett*, the recording of both punctuated by more odd behavior (he would play the same song entirely differently on each take, and he also once apparently bit a studio employee). During the recording of the Pink Floyd album *Wish You Were Here*, Syd turned up, although the band didn't recognize him. He announced he was ready to record his parts, then disappeared.

Now in his 60s, Syd is portly and bald and lives quietly in Cambridge. Every now and then he is tracked down by Floyd obsessives, and these encounters are said to leave him traumatized for days afterward.

It's a fine line between stupid and clever.

David Ivor St. Hubbins, Spinal Tap

Religious rockers

THEY'RE NOT ALL ON A HIGHWAY TO HELL, YOU KNOW

SONGS THAT MENTION GOD AND/OR JESUS

"The Sword of God" – Quasi
Song that seems to suggest much violence from the big fella
from our favorite Portland-based indie two-piece. Also the name
of the album.

"God" – Smashing Pumpkins
From the B-sides and *Rarities* album.

"God Is God" – Laibach
Oddball Slovenian antler-wearing types who like doing
off-the-wall cover versions.

"God Is on the Radio" – Queens of the Stone Age
Warning! Explicit lyrics!

"God Is Love" – Marvin Gaye
Marvin meant it. His dad was a preacher. Hold on,
didn't Mr. Gaye Sr. shoot his son dead with a gun?

"Personal Jesus" – Depeche Mode
Reach out and touch him!

"Hard On for Jesus" – The Dandy Warhols
Courtney Taylor praises God in his own way.

"Jesus Hairdo" – The Charlatans
Cheeky baggy scamps with their catchy organ-driven riffs.

"Black Jesus" – Ghostface Killah
Scary guy from rap outfit Wu-Tang Clan.

"The Lord's Prayer" – Siouxsie & the Banshees
Fourteen minutes of impro punk screeching with
Sid Vicious on drums. This is where it all started.

"Jesus Suck" – The Jesus and Mary Chain
Hairspray Scottish brothers make provocative
statements of blunt cool. With added feedback.

"My Sweet Lord" – George Harrison
Got done for plagiarizing the tune from the Chiffons'
1962 hit "He's So Fine," though.

"God Save the Queen" – Sex Pistols
The record that offended the British establishment to its core.

THE GOD DISSERS

Rock stars beware: When it comes to dealing with God—or rather, God's fans—it's best to think before you speak. John Lennon lived to regret his off-the-cuff (and probably factually accurate) comment that the Beatles were bigger than Jesus, forced as he was into making a public apology as he watched thousands of deranged American Christians and Ku Klux Klansmen burn his band's albums. It was the end of the Beatles' mass popularity in mainstream America, although, as George Harrison sagely noted: "They have to buy them before they can burn them."

Sinead O'Connor all but immolated her career back in 1992 in one moment on American TV's *Saturday Night Live* when she ripped in half a picture of Pope John Paul II. The TV network received thousands of complaints and was actually fined $2.5 million for this outbreak of blasphemy. The devil may have the best tunes, but it still doesn't do to diss God.

THE GOOD CHRISTIANS

Flying the flag for God has its own pitfalls. Who'd want to be tarred with the Cliff Richard brush, after all? Famous Christian hair band Stryper were a lonely Christian voice in the American heavy metal scene of the 1980s, while mid-1990s indie also-rans "Delirious?" were all that could be mustered by the God-fearing rock fan in the UK. But there has always been U2, a rare example of a critically acclaimed, vastly popular band with a fairly overt Christian message. Bono described their Elevation tour as being "more about Jesus than Elvis," and quoted Ecclesiastes to a journalist while playing them the *Zooropa* album. But then, U2 have always brought along a wry humanism and, probably more importantly, an intelligence to their rock 'n' roll worshipfulness. And anyway, not all the band are Christians (or Irish)—bass player Adam Clayton is not a member of any church, and he was born in Oxfordshire. More recently, the Killers turned out to have a Mormon singer (he doesn't like talking about it, though), Prince became a Jehovah's Witness, and talking about God seemed like less of an embarrassment, rather an assertion of one's cultural identity, in this religiously radicalized post-9/11 world.

THE MAHARISHI, SUBUH, AND DIONYSUS

When religion fever broke out in the rock star elite of the 1960s, Mick Jagger and girlfriend Marianne Faithfull went to India with the Beatles to spend what was supposed to be three months in 1968 studying Transcendental Meditation with the Maharishi. Joining them were Bob Dylan, Donovan, and Beach Boy Mike Love. The Beach Boys got so enthusiastic about the Maharishi that they announced a tour around the USA with him. Billed as "The Most Exciting Event of the Decade," it was a disaster. Tickets went unsold and the tour was abandoned after only three dates at a loss of $500,000.

The other guru whom the Beach Boys had encountered was Charles Manson, the hippie serial killer who carved a swastika into his forehead. Like Dennis Wilson's friendship with Manson, the Beach Boys' relationship with the Maharishi didn't last. Brian Wilson, the band's unstable genius, later tried on a new religion for size, Subuh, introduced to him by Roger McGuinn of the Byrds. Mick Jagger, meanwhile, who rejected the Maharishi as a fraud while in India, more recently claimed that the deity that most closely represents him is Dionysus, the Greek god of booze and having babies. Far more appropriate, we feel, for a man famous for singing "Sympathy for the Devil," banging every lady who would have him, and being charged with drug possession.

> **I have no belief in the Bible or religion, but I think Armageddon was a lucky guess. I honestly think it's going to happen.**
> George Michael

Bob Marley

Rastafarianism. He refused on religious grounds to receive treatment (amputation of a toe) for the malignant melanoma that eventually killed him.

The Shamen

Peddled a sort of techno Shamanism that blended the philosophies of psychedelic thinker Terrence McKenna with a kind of future (spelled *phuture*, by the way) tribalistic sci-fi hippie vision of Utopia, as experienced through repetitive beats from a Roland 808 drum machine and loads and loads of the killer rave drug Ecstasy.

Sir Bob Geldof

Because he was brought up a Catholic and taught by Christian brothers in Ireland, observers have wondered whether his reflexive philanthropic reaction to the plight of Africa is a result of his religious upbringing. He denies it and says he has rejected religion.

Sting

"I think I've always been fairly religious," says the Tantra-studying sex god. He was brought up a Catholic in an atmosphere where it was believed that "the best of us would become priests."

Arlo Guthrie

Folk star of the 1960s, Arlo Guthrie, son of Woody Guthrie, the folk musician who inspired Bob Dylan, became a Franciscan monk.

Jah Wobble

Former Public Image Limited bass player, now solo performer, is a self-professed "cockney mystic."

My religion is the Beatles.

Liam Gallagher

THE DEVIL INCARNATE

Once described as "the wickedest man in the world," Aleister Crowley (the notorious Devil-worshiping, drug-sucking, closet gay womanizing founder of the "religion" Thelema, who died in 1947) had quite a few musician admirers in that grim era of rock star decadence, the early 1970s. Probably the most notable of Crowley's ax-wielding acolytes was Led Zeppelin guitarist Jimmy Page, who famously bought Crowley's mansion, Boleskine House in Scotland, and has a large collection of Crowley memorabilia.

Page himself was rumored to dabble in black magic, and Zeppelin's massive success was often attributed to a spot of soul trading with the Devil. He wasn't the only artist said to have sold his soul to the cloven-hoofed chap in return for outstanding talent—that rock 'n' roll myth has been around since blues guitarist Son House started the rumor in the 1960s that guitar virtuoso Robert Johnson had exchanged his soul for his talent.

Ozzy Osbourne, formerly of Black Sabbath (who made a myth and a mint out of wearing upside-down crosses and all manner of arcane "dark forces" paraphernalia) also announced his appreciation of Crowley in his song "Mr. Crowley." Crowley is also one of the faces on the cover of the Beatles album *Sgt. Pepper's Lonely Heart's Club Band* and has been mentioned in songs by artists as diverse as Graham Bond (who developed the theory that he was Crowley's bastard son and then threw himself under a train in 1974), David Bowie (on "Quicksand"), Marilyn Manson (now, there's a surprise), and dusty 1980s goth rockers Fields of the Nephilim.

Even Michael Jackson is thought to have gotten in on the act. It's widely believed that the drawing of the old chap on the cover of Jacko's 1991 album *Dangerous* is none other than Aleister "The Beast" Crowley himself. And you can even find people who will insist that the album has so-called backward-masking messages hidden in the singing. Just spin the album backward (dig out the turntable and vinyl, kids, you can't do this on an iPod!) and you, too, like several hundred half-wits before you, might be able to imagine you can hear Jacko singing: "Come on. Yeah, Satan, yeah, just like me exact!"

JERRY LEE LEWIS: THE KILLER, TOO WEAK FOR JESUS

The conflict between rock 'n' roll and Christianity has been there since rock 'n' roll began, and it is embodied in Jerry Lee Lewis. Even when he was recording the rock 'n' roll classic "Great Balls of Fire," Lewis was in agonies trying to reconcile being a Christian with being a rock 'n' roller. Caught on tape, during the sessions recording the song, is a theological debate between Lewis and the session's producer, Sam Phillips. Phillips, trying to talk Lewis into accepting that rock 'n' roll can be a force for good, says: "You can save people." Lewis replies: "No! No! No! No! No! How can the Devil save souls? What are you talking about?" Lewis then went to live a life of debauchery, punctuated by bouts of remorse. Two wives and one son died. He took drugs and drank so much that he need a bottle of tequila in order to *sober up* to play gigs. In 1979, the TV evangelist Jimmy Swaggart pulled a raving Jerry Lee Lewis off stage, took him home, got rid of all the booze and drugs, and looked after him for a week. "I guess it saved my life," said Lewis.

BEATLES' BELIEFS

In 1965, George Harrison discovered the sitar, the Indian stringed instrument he recorded for the first time on *Rubber Soul*'s "Norwegian Wood." Toward the end of 1966, eager to learn more about the instrument, and bothered by the emerging tensions within the band, George went to India to study with sitar ace Ravi Shankar, an experience that excited his interest in Indian culture and religion. In 1967, he and the other Beatles attended a weekend retreat given in Wales by visiting guru Maharishi Mahesh Yogi, who was peddling a Westerner-friendly brand of Hindu-lite via his own Transcendental Meditation technique.

While the Beatles were in Wales, their manager Brian Epstein died. The Beatles looked to the Maharishi for consolation, and thus was forged a relationship with Eastern mysticism that lasted a few months for the Beatles (they wrote much of *The White Album* while in Rishikesh with the Maharishi in early 1968; they left when the guru allegedly tried to molest the actress Mia Farrow), but was the beginning of a lifelong devotion to the Hare Krishna movement for George.

POP STAR APOSTASIES! (THAT'S SWAPPING FAITHS, BY THE WAY)

Alice Cooper
Born-again Christian.
Bob Dylan
Now a born-again Christian
(formerly Jewish), released a dull
album about him and God called
(yawn) *Saved.*
Evanescence
Christian rockers turned secular. Had
the worldwide hit "Bring Me to Life"
in 2003, then renounced their
Christian background. Punished with
critical and commercial failure.
Boy George
Ex-Catholic-turned-Hare-Krishna.
Michael Jackson
Brought up Jehovah's Witness, now
believes in Neverland.
Madonna
Catholic-turned-kabbalah, a subsect
of Jewish mysticism. Her new
kabbalah name is Esther. Some
rabbis call kabbalah "crackpot," and
it is notorious for separating its
followers from their cash.
Hank Marvin
The bespectacled guitar hero of the
Shadows became a Jehovah's
Witness in 1973 from a previously
undecided stance.

Roger McGuinn
Born-again Christian (via Subuh).
Britney Spears
Madonna-wannabe, ergo also
a kabbalah devotee, converted
from regular Christianity, with
a tinge of born-again-ness.
**Jimmy Page, Robert Plant, John
Bonham (Led Zeppelin)**
According to legend, sold souls to
Devil in return for success. Bassist
John Paul Jones still owns his own
soul. John Bonham died in 1980.
Prince
Born a Seventh Day Adventist,
now a Jehovah's Witness.
Johnny Rotten
Brought up Catholic, briefly
reckoned himself (in song, at least)
to be an antichrist. Not *the*
Antichrist, though.
Cat Stevens
Rejected all music in 1978 when he
converted to Islam. Sold his guitars
and everything. Now he is playing
music again. And getting deported
from America. Oh, the irony.
Pete Townshend (the Who)
In 1969, he became an adherent of
Indian guru Meher Baba.

I feel closer to God when I am sexually aroused.
Prince

GURUS

Meher Baba
Provided spiritual salvation for Pete Townshend (although he still became an alcoholic, and a heroin addict, and got divorced, during his 10-year guru vibe).

Timothy Leary
LSD guru of the 1960s became professor of the hippie scene via his LSD consciousness experiments. He came up with the mantra: *Turn on, tune in, drop out.* He ran for election in various US political bodies in the late 1960s and approached John Lennon to write a theme song for the campaign. Leary had a slogan: *Come together.* Lennon wrote "Come Together," but decided against giving it to Leary, especially since Leary had been locked up in prison.

Maharishi
Bearded loser with a taste for expensive cars and girls. Shot to fame as the Beatles' guru, and then was rejected by them when they suspected him of molesting girls.

Manamarhashi
Guru to the likes of John McLaughlin, the Yorkshire guitar whiz who played with Miles Davis.

McLaughlin named his post-Miles band the Mahavishnu Orchestra after his given Hindu name. Carlos Santana was another devotee.

Soka Gakkai International (SGI)
The Buddhist sect led by Daisaku Ikeda since 1975 has Stevie Wonder, Suzanne Vega, and another former Miles Davis band member, Herbie Hancock, among its membership.

Swami Prabhavananda
British intellectual and philosopher Aldous Huxley had his own guru in the shape of Swami Prabhavananda in the 1930s. In the 1950s, he took mescaline and then wrote *The Doors of Perception*, which was the book that gave Jim Morrison the name of his band and a lifestyle to follow. Huxley asked to be administered with a dose of LSD on his deathbed.

Swami Prabhupada
A Hindu guru who set about creating converts with a gig featuring the Grateful Dead, Big Brother and the Holding Company, Quicksilver Messenger Service, and Jefferson Airplane in San Francisco in 1967. Replaced the Maharishi as the Beatles' guru for a while.

ERIC CLAPTON

The graffito CLAPTON IS GOD was once a familiar sight on concrete bridges across the land. He earned the title by being quite good at playing the guitar, rather than by any discernible aura of deity. He did, however, enjoy an unlikely conversion to Christianity when two guys walked into his dressing room after a gig while he was touring with the short-lived supergroup Blind Faith in the USA in 1969. They asked if they could pray with him, and the three of them got down on their knees and did just that.

Clapton has said that he experienced a blinding light (could have been the cocaine, perhaps?) and then felt he wanted to show the two unnamed prayer guys a poster of Jimi Hendrix. The poster turned out to have an image of Jesus Christ on it. Gasp! This was the sign Eric needed to complete his miraculous conversion. In 1976, fat, drunk, and loaded on coke, horse, and all manner of rock pig intoxicants, he added his support to the racist rantings of Enoch Powell MP, saying that Britain was in danger of becoming a "black colony" (this from a man who made a career from ripping off black music). He then ran off with George Harrison's wife (marrying her in 1979, and then divorcing her in 1988). And they say that rock star religious conversions are mostly unconvincing.

> Christianity will go. It will vanish and shrink. I needn't argue about that; I'm right and I will be proved right. We are more popular than Jesus now. I don't know which will go first— rock 'n' roll or Christianity. Jesus was all right, but his disciples were thick and ordinary. It's them twisting it that ruins it for me.
>
> John Lennon—that "we're bigger than Jesus" quote in full from a 1966 interview he gave to the *Evening Standard*

Violently
unhappy

SEX AND DRUGS AND ROCK 'N' ROLL, AND *VIOLENCE*

VIOLENT TITLES

"Soba Violence" – Beastie Boys
"Vintage Violence" – John Cale
"Bottled Violence" – Minor Threat
"Violence" – Mott the Hoople
"Riot of Violence" – Napalm Death
"Violence" – Pet Shop Boys
"Domestic Violence" – RZA
"Sex & Violence" – Stone Temple Pilots
"The Violence of Truth" – The The

SID VICIOUS – LIVING UP TO HIS NAME

A violent atmosphere surrounded the Sex Pistols most of the time, and it regularly flared up around them. At the 100 Club Punk Festival in 1976, before he had even joined the band, Sid Vicious gave music journalist Nick Kent a nasty beating—with a bike chain. The next night, during a set by the Damned, Vicious threw a glass that shattered on a pillar and blinded a girl in one eye. When he joined the Sex Pistols, things only worsened. A mock fight with drummer Paul Cook at their signing ceremony with A&M Records turned real, and Sid traipsed blood through the record company's offices and then smashed up the toilets. Next, Vicious threatened veteran radio DJ and television presenter Bob Harris with a glass, and the band were thrown off A&M Records as a result. While on tour in America, Sid called an audience in a southern bar a "bunch of cowboy faggots" and, when one member came after him, used his bass guitar to club him down. In the end, Sid's violence led to the murder of his girlfriend Nancy Spungen at Manhattan's famous bohemian haven the Chelsea Hotel. He died of a heroin overdose before he could stand trial.

Violence isn't always evil. What's evil is the infatuation with violence.
Jim Morrison

LED ZEPPELIN

Headliners of so many rock legends, Led Zeppelin were renowned for their hardness. Or rather, the gangsterish, uncompromising attitude of their infamous manager, Peter Grant. A huge man, Grant would strike the fear of God into anyone who dared try to swindle the Zep out of a cent. He was notoriously hard on bootleggers, and once appeared at a record shop in London's Chancery Lane, turned the shop's OPEN sign around, and threatened the owner with all manner of terrifying bodily harm until he handed over his entire stock of Led Zeppelin bootlegs.

One time, in Canada, Grant spied a man in the crowd holding a microphone aloft at a show. He sent roadies out to pull the hapless chap backstage, where they smashed up his equipment. It turned out he was from the local council and was checking decibel levels. On the same tour, the band turned up to play a festival in Winnipeg. It was raining, and there was crowd trouble. The concert promoter approached Grant, gave him the band's fee, and told him that Led Zeppelin wouldn't be playing. Grant flew into a rage until the promoter explained that the band's New York agent had told him that if it was raining, the band wouldn't play, and if they didn't get paid for not playing, they'd break someone's legs.

GUNS AND AMMO

He invented the Wall of Sound and gave the world lush girl-pop hits in the 1960s and produced the post-split Beatles album *Let It Be*, but by the 1970s, Phil Spector's behavior was becoming famously erratic. During the recording sessions for the blighted 1973 John Lennon solo album *Rock 'n' Roll*, Spector became so enraged that he pulled out his gun and shot into the studio's ceiling. Spector was already on probation for a 1972 misdemeanor of carrying a loaded firearm in public. In 1975, he copped another two years' probation for brandishing a gun in a hotel in Hollywood. It was bound to end badly, and sure enough, in 2003 he was arrested for the murder of actress Lana Clarkson. He claimed that he shot her by accident, and then later that she committed suicide.

LOU AND DAVID

Lou Reed and David Bowie were pals in the 1970s. Bowie produced the breakthrough Lou Reed solo album *Transformer*, and the two were often seen out and about together enjoying the nightlife New York had to offer. They were even rumored to have "fallen in love." After all, Bowie had proclaimed himself bisexual, and Reed's sexuality was equally ambiguous. And they had been seen (more tellingly, *photographed*) kissing, too. But in 1979, relations suddenly soured between the two icons. At a restaurant in South Kensington, the two were apparently enjoying a reunion when suddenly Lou started battering Bowie. "Don't you *ever* say that to me again!" Lou is reported to have screamed after the first flurry of fists were exchanged. Then he calmed down, and the pair appeared to have made up. Within a few minutes, however, Lou started throwing punches again, shouting: "I told you never to say that!" He then left the restaurant, at which point Bowie started throwing tables around and breaking potted plants before storming out himself. The cause of Lou's rage has never been fully explained, although it seems to have had something to do with Bowie offering to produce Lou's next album, but only if he kicked drugs.

> **The violence between women is unbelievable. Women try to make each other crawl so that their knees are bleeding.**
> Tori Amos

IKE

Ike Turner's reputation never recovered from his propensity for violence toward his wife, Tina. According to Tina's autobiography, Ike was a controlling coke-addled monster who would beat her and burn her with cigarettes and coffee whenever he deemed that she'd "got out of hand." She eventually walked out on him in 1975, and Ike's decline was as rapid as it was predictable. He bankrupted himself snorting more cocaine, and his studio burned down in 1982. When Ike and Tina Turner were inducted into the Rock 'n' Roll Hall of Fame in 1991, Ike couldn't make the ceremony—unfortunately he was in prison.

ALTAMONT

The Rolling Stones were no strangers to rowdy gigs. Back in 1964, their first tour of the USA ended with a riot at Carnegie Hall, and when they embarked on a UK tour shortly after their return, a gig in Blackpool erupted into violence. Some 50 fans ended up hospitalized, all the band's equipment was wrecked by the rampaging crowd, a grand piano was smashed to pieces, and chandeliers were wrenched from the ceiling. There were more riots in Belfast and Holland, trouble in Manchester and Jersey, and in Paris 150 were arrested after going bonkers in the foyer and the streets outside the Olympia Theatre. In Australia, fans were crushed at Sydney Airport when overenthusiastic crowds got out of hand. But worse than all of these was the Altamont gig in December 1969. Hell's Angels had been hired to police the 30,000-strong crowd. They were paid in booze, and soon things got out

of hand. One Angel punched Jefferson Airplane's singer Marty Balin unconscious on stage. They then started attacking festivalgoers who grew restless when Jefferson Airplane stopped playing. The Grateful Dead decided not to play, causing more tension, and by the time the Stones came on stage, the atmosphere was tense. Hell's Angels then attacked a young man called Meredith Hunter. They later testified that he'd pulled out a gun. A gun was never found, but the Angels beat Hunter to death with pool cues and fists. He was also hit with bike chains and stabbed five times. There were three other deaths at Altamont: A car drove into a campfire and killed two people, and another man died after falling into a nearby canal. This concert is thought to signal the day the 1960s hippie dream died, and the dawning of a new, dark era of violence.

Lots of people were tired and tempers were frayed.
Keith Richards, about Altamont

gods of rock

OTHER SPECTACULAR ACTS OF VIOLENCE

Al Green's girlfriend
Asked Al to marry her, he said no, she threw a pan of boiling grits on him when he was naked in the shower and then committed suicide. Al turned to God after this appalling event.

Arthur Lee
Seminal figure of LA's mid-1960s psychedelic rock scene. After breaking into an ex-girlfriend's apartment and trying to set it aflame in 1995, he was arrested in 1996 for shooting a gun into the air during an argument with a neighbor. He was convicted and served nearly 6 years of a 12-year sentence.

Lisa "Left Eye" Lopes
Burned a house down in a fit of rage after her football star boyfriend's late night out with the boys.

Courtney Love
Struck LA celeb journalist Belissa Cohen at a 1998 fashion show after Cohen tried to snap a photo of her. As she aimed her camera, Love went ballistic, whacked her in the face, and yelled: "Don't be taking pictures of me! Do you think I'm not still punk rock?"

Ozzy Osbourne
Tried to strangle his wife, Sharon, and threatened to kill her. He was arrested, but charges were dropped at her insistence. Sharon commented that if she'd had a gun she would probably have shot him. Cuddly Ozzy blames the drugs.

The Stranglers
Regularly beat up music journalists, particularly bass player Jean-Jacques Burnel, but they met their match in Sweden, when they were assailed by the local punk-hating gang known as Raggere.

Jack White
The increasingly erratic Jack White of the White Stripes was busted for aggravated assault in 2003 when he repeatedly punched singer Jason Stollsteimer of fellow Detroit band the Von Bondies.

THE GREAT FEEDBACK RIOTS OF 1985

The Jesus and Mary Chain, the legendary indie band formed by brothers Jim and William Reid, with Primal-Scream-in-waiting Bobby Gillespie on drums, were enjoying success in the mid-1980s thanks to their feedbacking rock 'n' roll hymns like the incendiary debut single "Upside Down." Also part of the irresistible package were the riots that their gigs became famous for, mainly inspired by the antagonism between the two brothers. Their biggest riot happened in March 1985 at the North London Polytechnic. The support band had already wound up the crowd by throwing a bottle at them, and the crowd was ready for a ruckus knowing that the riots were part of the show, inspired in part by the band's surly attitude (they'd play with their backs to the audience and abuse any nearby members of the music press). When the band finally appeared, they played for less than 20 minutes, and much of that was feedback. When they left the stage the crowd ripped the place apart. "Sometimes we only played for nine minutes," recalled Jim Reid nostalgically a couple of years later. The band finally split up in 1999 after the brothers fell out with each other on stage.

> **I hate to advocate drugs, alcohol, violence, or insanity to anyone, but they've always worked for me.**
> Hunter S. Thompson

WHO LEFT THE SEAT UP?

In 1988, James Brown came back to his office building, tired and emotional (translation: on drugs), to find someone had used his private bathroom. Enraged, he threatened a roomful of people (who were innocently enjoying an insurance seminar, of all things) with a shotgun and then went on the run. Police chased him for six miles, and were finally able to arrest him only after they shot out the tires of Brown's car. The Godfather of Soul served two years of a six-year jail sentence for that transgression, where he had to share more than just the bathroom.

gods of rock

LENNONS

The cuddly Fab Four image of the Beatles belied the reality of the band's history. John Lennon was famed for his violent temper, and fights were a common fact of life in Liverpool's rough dance halls and in Hamburg's even rougher clubs. Lennon was involved in his share. According to the controversial biographer Albert Goldman, during the band's Hamburg days, Lennon had a fight with his friend and the band's original bass player Stu Sutcliffe. Lennon believed this fight may have caused the blood clot in his brain that killed him. Certainly, during Lennon's so-called lost weekend, 18 months when he and Yoko were living apart in the early 1970s, he was regularly in the gossip columns for being drunk and fighting, often in the company of another legendary brawler, Harry Nilsson. One spectacular public ding-dong was at the LA Troubadour where Lennon had been heckling the band, the Smothers Brothers. The band's manager came over to shut Lennon up, and all hell broke loose. The fighting spilled out into the parking lot, and in the mêlée a photographer got hit in the eye. She later sued Lennon. It seems that John's son Sean might have inherited some of his dad's punchiness. At the "All Tomorrow's Parties" event in 2005, he allegedly tried to pick a fight with Jayne County's bass player. "Security had to separate them, or blood would have spilled," Jayne told reporters.

RICK JAMES

The funk superstar was Motown's biggest-selling act in the late 1970s and early 1980s. He was one of the first stars to adopt the cornrow braided hairdo that is now so popular. His mega-hit "Super Freak" was later sampled by MC Hammer for Hammer's mega-hit "U Can't Touch This." However, a decline into crack cocaine addiction in the late 1980s led to his arrest in 1991 for false imprisonment and torture. A woman had stolen an ounce of crack from him, and alleged that he punished her by burning her on the legs and stomach with a hot crack pipe, and forced her to have sex with his girlfriend (who was also charged). In 1993, he was jailed for two years for assaulting another woman. According to the prosecution, he bound and beat the woman in a hotel room for 12 hours. James died in 2004 from a heart attack.

BATTLING BJORK

In a roundup of rock 'n' roll kickings, the name Bjork isn't one you'd necessarily expect to encounter. However, the Icelandic songbird lost her rag quite spectacularly at Bangkok International Airport in 1996. The cause? It looked innocuous enough: television journalist Julie Kaufman holding a microphone and saying: "Welcome to Bangkok, Bjork." Unfortunately, Bjork didn't take the welcome very well, and in moments was swinging the hapless reporter around by her hair, shouting obscenities, and generally giving as good a roughing-up as she could muster. It was all caught on film. Later, Bjork apologized and said she was trying to protect her son from media attention, something she spectacularly failed to achieve; the clip was beamed around the world for days. This was at a time in Bjork's life when she was mixed up in an unpleasant (and, frankly, mystifying) love triangle with Tricky and Goldie, each of them famed for a tendency toward the thuggish.

BIG MOUTH STRIKES AGAIN

Liam and Noel Gallagher's fighting has long been the stuff of legend. One altercation, caught on tape at a press conference by a music journalist, was immortalized when it was released as a single called "Sibling Rivalry." In the press conference, Noel accused Liam of behaving like a hooligan. In 1996, violence stalked the band's tours. Liam was pulled out of a fight with a fan at a show in the UK, which then turned into a riot, and just two weeks later, an American tour ended in near disaster when the brothers' arguments escalated into violence. In 1997, Liam was cautioned for a road rage incident (he grabbed a cyclist through the window of his Mercedes and dragged him along with the car). Wherever Liam went, fisticuffs were never far behind, whether it was a Swiss music festival where he goaded the audience into a near riot, his public row with Robbie Williams (who challenged Liam to a fight at the 2000 Brit Awards), or an alleged assault on a British Airways flight in 2001. Since Liam got his two front teeth knocked out in a nightclub fight in Munich in 2002, causing Oasis to postpone several shows, he seems to have been less eager to provoke trouble.

gods of rock

GUN LOVERS

50 Cent
Always getting arrested for something or other, usually involving guns.

Kurt Cobain
Photographed many times brandishing guns shortly before his
gun-assisted suicide.

David Crosby
A hotel employee found cannabis and a gun in his room in 2003. In 1985, he
served a year in prison for cocaine and gun violations.

Eminem
Arrested twice on firearms violations.

Flavor Flav
Arrested for alleged gun totin' in 1993.

Ice-T
Gun collector and former LA gang member.

Jerry Lee Lewis
Shot his bass player in the chest accidentally in 1976. Was arrested again a
few weeks later when he turned up at Elvis's house Graceland, showed the
security guard his gun, and said he'd come to "kill Elvis."

Ted Nugent
Unapologetic gun-loving redneck monster.

Puff Daddy
Arrested for illegal possession of a firearm in 2000.

Phil Spector
Oh dear.

> **Everyone knows that if you've got a brother,
> you're going to fight.**
> Liam Gallagher

The rise of the machines

NO DANCE MUSIC, NO HIP-HOP,
NO DURAN DURAN—CAN WE IMAGINE A
WORLD WITHOUT THE SYNTHESIZER?

WITHOUT SYNTHESIZERS, THERE'D BE NO . . .

"Blue Monday" – New Order

"Can't Get You Out of My Head" – Kylie Minogue

"Don't You Want Me" – Human League

"Jump" – Van Halen

"Material Girl" – Madonna

"Mr. Blue Sky" – Electric Light Orchestra

"Take on Me" – A-Ha

"Rio" – Duran Duran

"Superstition" – Stevie Wonder

"Thriller" – Michael Jackson

"West End Girls" – Pet Shop Boys

BOB MOOG

The synth revolution was a long time coming. Bob Moog, a Cornell University graduate, started out selling theremin kits (they make the haunting ghostly noise much used in 1950s sci-fi movies and by the Beach Boys in "Good Vibrations"). Then he developed a synthesizer. Thanks to the vast success of Wendy Carlos's *Switched-On Bach* album in 1969, Moog had back orders for his complex (and expensive) modular system from other record companies that wanted to crank out "Moog music" and make a quick buck. But these records mostly flopped; by 1970, the orders had dried up and the company was in trouble. It had money pumped into it by a financier who moved the company to Buffalo, New York, to an old gelatin factory. "Every kook and crazy in the area had a job there," remembered Moog, "because you had to be nuts to work in a place like that." For 100 years, the building had been creating a stink for 10 miles around, boiling buffalo hides in vats and extracting gelatin. And so Moog's pristine Minimoog synthesizers, the "sound of the future" and loved by rock star keyboard players, were produced in "a smelly, damp, uncomfortable, unattractive, unfinished hole that we worked in from 1971 to 1974." Moog passed away in 2005, four months after being diagnosed with a brain tumor.

THE FIRST SYNTHESIZER?

The world's first-ever synthesizer was made by the American inventor Thaddeus Cahill. At great expense, but with little reward, Thaddeus built his Telharmonium (aka the Dyna-mophone) in 1895. Made of mechanical motors and telephone receivers, but played from a keyboard, it wasn't until 1906 that it was successfully demonstrated. Its main problem was that it weighed 200 tons and cost in excess of $200,000 to build. It actually used the telephone system as part of its amplification, and performances would be broadcast through telephones so loudly that you didn't have to pick the phone up to listen. Thaddeus tried to sell his machines to hotels, the idea being that they could play soothing music into every room. Impressive demonstrations of the technology failed to sell any of his machines, and it is thought that the last machine (only three were built) was broken up and dumped in the Hudson River in the 1950s. No recordings of Telharmonium music were ever made.

ZAPPLE — THE BEATLES AND ELECTRONIC MUSIC

In the late 1960s, the Beatles had so much money that they started throwing quite a bit of it away. One loss-making enterprise followed another; the Apple boutique, Apple Records (this was, of course, turned around and continues to this day), and the Apple sublabel, Zapple. Zapple was intended as the outlet for all the Beatles' sonic experiments. The Fab Four had been early enthusiasts of electronic music synthesizers and the sound collage techniques pioneered by the likes of Stockhausen. *The White Album* had the experimental "Revolution 9" taking up a bewildering eight minutes of proceedings, and the album *Abbey Road* featured a Moog synthesizer (on George's "Here Comes the Sun" and "Because"). George was so enamored of the Moog synthesizer he'd been playing around with that he released an entire album of his synthy noodlings called *Electronic Sound* on the newly established Zapple label. Also released on Zapple (on the same day as *Electronic Sound*, May 7, 1969) was *Unfinished Music No. 2: Life with the Lions* by John and Yoko. Zapple was shut down before a third release, a matter of only a few weeks after it was launched.

gods of rock

ESSENTIAL ELECTRONIC MUSIC ALBUMS

Oxygene – Jean Michel Jarre
A fluid synthesizer masterpiece, released in 1978.

Computer World – Kraftwerk
They reached electronic perfection with this album in 1981, though *Autobahn*, *Man Machine*, *Radioactivity*, and *Trans-Europe Express* are all excellent, too.

Yellow Magic Orchestra – Yellow Magic Orchestra
The Japanese trio who featured Ryuichi Sakamoto (who also scored the film *Merry Christmas, Mr. Lawrence*) are electronic music pioneers and this, their first album from 1978, is a classic.

Dare – Human League
Synth pop glory, stuffed with hit singles, that sold millions of copies in 1981.

Penthouse and Pavement – Heaven 17
When two members split from the Human League, they formed Heaven 17 and released this excellent album in 1981. They also retained royalties on the next Human League album as part of the deal for allowing them to continue to use the name. That probably made them more money than their own album.

Phaedra – Tangerine Dream
This 1973 album is one of over 70 to choose from, but is widely believed to be TD's best.

Subliminal Sandwich – Meat Beat Manifesto
The sound of classic synths being put through their paces by one of the best knob twiddlers currently making records.

> When synthesizers came along, it was the first time I thought that the two things I loved, which were science and music, could be put together.
>
> **Herbie Hancock**

KRAFTWERK — GERMANS INVENT HIP-HOP BY MISTAKE

The Beach Boys of electronic music? Kraftwerk is the life's work of two men: Florian Schneider and Ralf Hütter. They met in the 1960s while studying at the Dusseldorf Conservatory (flute and organ, respectively), but soon gave up their classical studies to pursue experimental music. Their first release was with the band Organization in 1970, a difficult album called *Tone Float*, full of blurty noises and incoherent jamming, which came in the wake of other German bands like Can and Amon Düül bagging record deals. The debut Kraftwerk album appeared in the same year, but it wasn't until 1974 and the release of *Autobahn*, their fourth album, that the breakthrough came. From the opening notes of the smooth, bouncing synthesizer bass line and the trance-inducing melody and singing, this truly was future music. It sounded like nothing else. Previously, synthesizers had been used mostly to squeal like guitars during solos, or to emulate classical instruments. Here, they were being employed for their own aesthetic. An edited version of the 22-minute track "Autobahn" gave Kraftwerk a huge hit single in the UK, and the album was rightly hailed as a classic. They followed it with four more albums (*Radioactivity*, *Trans-Europe Express*, *Man Machine*, and *Computer World*), which among them defined the sound palette for most electronic music to come, including hip-hop (invented by Afrika Bambaataa by using two turntables to mix elements of *Trans-Europe Express* and *Computer World*) and techno, not to mention most contemporary pop music and the technology used to produce it. Over the last 20 years, Kraftwerk have released only two bona fide new studio albums, and have toured rarely. They remain one of the most influential bands in the world, and one of the most enigmatic.

> I remember well that we played in Paris on 110 volts and all the tempos were out of tune. At 8 PM the big factories that plug into the network were making the voltage fluctuate. Peugeot were making our tempos change.
> Ralf Hütter, Kraftwerk

gods of rock

THEY ALSO SERVED

Vince Clarke: Left Depeche Mode after one album and went on to dominate the UK and US charts with Yazoo and then Erasure, who are still very popular.

Depeche Mode: Started out in Essex with the bouncy hit "Just Can't Get Enough," then got massive in America. Singer Dave Gahan nearly killed himself with heroin. He's better now. Probably the main inspiration for US techno. They've had more than 30 hit singles in the UK.

Howard Jones: Big, very big, in 1983, this synth solo act spiced things up with a dancer who would perform literal interpretations of the songs. Anyone who can remember him imploring watchers of *Top of the Pops* to "throw off your mental chains" knows what we mean.

OMD: Fantastically pretentious band name (Orchestral Manoeuvres in the Dark) and some groundbreaking electronic records in the late 1970s led to some very big hits in the 1980s. OMD's Andy McCluskey went on to be the "brains" behind pop sensations Atomic Kitten.

Thompson Twins: A string of hits in the early 1980s, but not really pioneers.

Ultravox: After John Foxx left and became a solo synth star, Ultravox brought in Midge Ure and went total synth, too, and landed the giant synth hit "Vienna."

Visage: Better at makeup than records, but their debut 45, "Fade to Grey," is a classic genre piece.

THE SYNTHESIZER RECORD BREAKER

French synthesizer superstar Jean Michel Jarre, son of movie soundtrack composer Maurice Jarre, made his name with his debut album *Oxygene* in 1976. An album of fluid and organic synthesizer music, it sold by the truckload. Jarre also possesses the distinction of appearing in the *Guinness Book of Records* for attracting an enormous crowd (in excess of one million) for his outdoor gig at La Place de la Concorde in Paris in 1979. He trumped his own record in 1986 when he played to 1.5 million people at a concert in Houston and again in 1990 when 2.5 million showed up to hear him play in Paris. In 1997, a gig in Moscow broke the record once again, this time attracting a crowd of 3.5 million. He has sold 72 million albums, which makes him one of the most successful purveyors of electronic music of all time, and the 74th best-selling artist in the world.

TANGERINE DREAM — THE ORIGINAL CATHEDRAL OF SOUND

The Tangs, as they were affectionately called by their devotees for a while in the 1970s, occupy a peculiar place in the history of electronic music. They were the first of the wave of German bands to be identified as a purely synthesizer band. They were formed in 1967 by Edgar Froese, Klaus Schulze, and Conrad Schnitzler. At first, they were a fairly standard rock outfit, but under Schnitzler's guidance, they became a synth band, allowing the machines to provide all the rhythms. As a result, their music pulsed and throbbed, and was washed with synth atmospheres. It was warm, ambient, and suitably trippy for the LSD generation, who flocked to the gigs. The Tangs sought unusual venues for gigs, and became known for their affinity for playing in cathedrals. This, perhaps, is where the music journalism cliché *cathedrals of sound* was forged. For a donation of 4,000 francs, a French promoter was able to secure Rheims Cathedral in northwest France for a show in 1974. Some 6,000 people showed up to the 3,000-capacity cathedral, and when they needed to pee, there weren't many bathrooms. You can imagine the horror. The Vatican banned the band from performing on church property ever again and demanded that the cathedral be reconsecrated. Thus was sealed the Tang's rep as a heavy freak-out experience.

WALTER/WENDY CARLOS

One of the most important innovators in the world of modern electronic music was Walter Carlos. Walter had gender reassignment surgery in 1972 and became Wendy, but far more important is the fact that her first album, 1969's *Switched-On Bach*, a collection of synthesized versions of Bach's greatest hits, so to speak, became the first-ever album of classical music to be awarded a platinum disc. The big picture on the cover of an astronaut might have helped. Before recording that electronic blockbuster, she worked with Bob Moog, the father of the modern synthesizer, on his early projects. Another of Carlos's great achievements was the soundtrack for Stanley Kubrick's controversial film *A Clockwork Orange*. She also scored Kubrick's horror classic *The Shining*.

GREAT SYNTHS AND THEIR FAMOUS FANS

Minimoog
The classic. Bob Moog (pronounced *mogue*) gave his name to the machine that, for a while, was synonymous with the word *synthesizer*. Hear it on *Abbey Road* by the Beatles, and a great deal of 1970s rock music, including many Pink Floyd albums. The Minimoog is still used by the Prodigy, Nine Inch Nails, and Stereolab.

ARP 2600
This machine is used today by the likes of the Chemical Brothers, Depeche Mode, Underworld, and Marilyn Manson, and was used in the 1970s by Joy Division and John Lennon.

Roland Jupiter 8
Japanese electronics company Roland was started in 1972 and remains one of the most successful electronic music companies in the world. Their Jupiter 8 synth was *the* sound of the 1980s New Romantics and the one you'd see most often on *Top of the Pops*, played by boys with bangs like Duran Duran (especially on "Rio") and Depeche Mode. Still used by Blur, Pet Shop Boys, and Underworld.

Korg MS20
Looks like something off *Dr. Who*. Sounded like it, too. Used when it came out (1978–1982) by the likes of Blancmange. Used today by Air, the Beastie Boys, and Aphex Twin.

Yamaha CS-80
This is the monster that Stevie Wonder liked so much. It cost almost $9,000 when it first came out in 1978, and another $500 to get the thing tuned. ELO had one, and so did Paul McCartney. Not many people use them these days, perhaps mainly because they weigh more than a house.

EDP Wasp
Made by a small UK company, the Wasp boasted a yellow-and-black keyboard, as did the Gnat, the smaller version. They also brought out a machine called the Spider. And another called the Caterpillar. Then they went bust.

WHO WAS STOCKHAUSEN, ANYWAY?

Karlheinz Stockhausen is a name that is muttered by electronic musicians in reverential whispers. Kraftwerk went to see one of his concerts in Germany in the late 1960s (off their heads on LSD), and came away determined to create a new music influenced by what they'd experienced. Paul McCartney was a big fan, and put Stockhausen on the cover of the *Sgt. Pepper* album. Members of Tangerine Dream studied under him.

Stockhausen (b. 1928) is a composer who is interested in the psychological and acoustic properties of music, rather than its melodic tradition. Okay? Still with us? The next bit's confusing, too, but there's a good anecdote after it, so bear with us. In his attempts to explore this abstract and intellectual approach to music, Stockhausen wrote pieces of music in the 1950s ("Punkte," "Kontra-Punkte," and "Kreuzspiel"), which set the sounds of orchestras

against one another. The 1959 piece "Gruppen" needs three orchestras to chuck out a series of notes at each other, so the audience gets to experience the sound flying around.

Stockhausen then wanted to see what effects gravity has on sound, and set about trying to develop a way of suspending and swinging musicians around on ropes. The most extreme expression of this idea came in 1993 when he wrote "Helikopter-Streichquartett," where members of a string quartet play their parts while they hover above the venue in four helicopters. The audience in the venue listen to the performance through speakers, together with the sound of the helicopters. It's this sense of thinking about the acoustic properties of sound itself, rather than the resulting music, that had such a huge impact on adventurous pop music. So *that's* who Karlheinz Stockhausen is then.

We liked ABBA. We wanted to *be* ABBA.

Phil Oakey, the Human League

MOST NOTABLE SYNTH STAR HAIRCUTS

Phil Oakey (Human League): Two haircuts in one—one side of long, flowing locks like some heavy metal guy, the other, a nice short back and sides.

Michael Score (A Flock of Seagulls): Possibly the most famous hairdo in synth pop, a coiffure that suggested to many an actual seagull in flight.

Gary Numan: Sported a David Bowie (c. 1976) for several years. Dyed it blue for a duet with Leo Sayer.

Alannah Currie (Thompson Twins): A huge pile of tight ringlets tumbling out from under a peaked cap perched on her head at a jaunty angle. The 1980s summed up in one hairdo.

Nick Beggs (Kajagoogoo): He played bass, but the haircut (puffball on top, straggly beaded braids down the back) was a new romantic 1980s behemoth.

METAL MACHINE MUSIC

Lou Reed, formerly of New York's Andy Warhol–backed art rock outfit the Velvet Underground, thought he'd have a stab at making some of that there electronic music. It was 1975, and many say that the heroin-addicted transgressive and belligerent icon of cool was desperate to get out of his record deal at the time. That's why, it is thought, he delivered to RCA the double album *Metal Machine Music*, four sides of unlistenable screaming feedback and racket that he called "an instrumental electronic composition"— he has since claimed it was a serious piece of music that includes bits of Beethoven's *Pastoral* and *Eroica*.

So convinced were RCA that this was an important piece of contemporary classical music, they suggested releasing it on their Red Seal label, their classical music imprint. It sold around 150,000 when it was first released, and a good proportion of those were returned by irate fans. Lou remains better known for his work with the Velvet Underground, the single "Walk on the Wild Side" and the tune "Perfect Day," which was used as a BBC signature tune, despite being a song about heroin.

HOW THE SAMPLER CHANGED MUSIC

What is a sampler? Simply put, it's a machine that allows you to take any sound and play it back from a keyboard. So you can have an entire orchestra at your fingertips, or a chorus of barking dogs. You can also slice and loop beats with a sampler, and this is the technique employed by hip-hop and dance music.

The first widely used instrument capable of sampling was the Mellotron. It used a complex mechanical system of tape loops to produce wobbly string sounds, and its distinctive tones can be heard most famously on the Beatles' "Strawberry Fields Forever." In the 1980s, the computer age gave the music world the Fairlight sampler. Invented by two Australians, it was used only by the most wealthy of pop stars; Stevie Wonder, Kate Bush, and Peter Gabriel were early adopters. Its $45,000 price tag

(for a basic model, $90,000 for the full monty) was too much for most musicians.

Other companies introduced sampling technology through the 1980s, but it was the legendary Akai S900, launched in 1985, that changed everything forever. No recording studio was complete without an Akai, and it was this machine that enabled Vanilla Ice to sample the opening bass line from the Queen/David Bowie hit "Under Pressure" for his "Ice Ice Baby," the Verve to sample the Rolling Stones for their "Bittersweet Symphony" and for countless dance acts to steal a New Order bass drum sound.

Nowadays, the average $800 home computer is capable of doing everything an Akai and a Fairlight could.

> **I'm struck by the insidious, computer-driven tendency to take things out of the domain of muscular activity and put them into the domain of mental activity.**
> **Brian Eno**

gods of rock

THE COMPOSER OF ONE OF THE MOST-HEARD PIECES OF MUSIC

Brian Eno started out as Roxy Music's electronics wizard, twiddling synthesizers and manipulating tape machines to give the band a sci-fi edge. He left the band in 1973 to forge a career as a solo artist and as a producer. In the 1970s, he made two enormous contributions to pop music: He developed ambient music (with his album *Music for Airports* in 1978), and he co-wrote and produced three of David Bowie's most important albums, *Low*, *Heroes*, and *Lodger*.

His production credits include the best albums by some of the most influential artists in music, and when he came to produce U2's 1984 album *The Unforgettable Fire*, he gave them a new lease on life. The six Eno-produced U2 albums have sold 70 million copies. One Eno composition was heard every day by millions upon millions of listeners (110 million bought it), although it is now never heard. He was paid $35,000 to compose the start-up music for the Windows 95 operating system.

REAL FUTURISTS DON'T WEAR MAKEUP

The Futurists of London, around 1980, were makeup-wearing boys and girls who were a part of a distinctly modernist fashion and music movement. The scene was centered on a club in London called Blitz, and the music they liked was the cool, synthesizer tones of bands like Visage, the Human League, Depeche Mode, and Spandau Ballet.

By calling themselves Futurists, though, they were harking back 70 years to the first Futurists, who were also interested in music made by machines. These slightly crackers Italian thinkers and artists came up with the *Technical Manifesto of Futurist Music* pamphlet in 1911, perhaps the real start of electronic music.

The Italian Futurists believed that music needed to reflect the modernity and cacophony of modern cities, and so set about inventing noisemaking machines like the Howler and the Burster to prove their point. They also unfortunately allied themselves to Italian fascism.

The dark pleasures of prog

THE GAPING BLACK HOLE
BETWEEN THE BEATLES AND PUNK

An English attempt in the 1960s to combine rock with classical music and jazz fusion, prog (aka progressive rock) was mainly the fault of a handful of posh British hippies who listened to classical works by the likes of Stravinsky and Vivaldi and considered themselves proper musicians. Most wanted to introduce a symphonic vibe into psychedelia; some, like Keith Emerson, were mostly interested in playing immense solos to show off how good they were at playing their organ/guitar/drums/flute.

Spotting prog isn't too tricky: Anything that is rock music but is plundering classical music (although isn't a musical by Andrew Lloyd Webber) is likely to be prog. Any rock album with a track that lasts more than around eight minutes is *likely* to be prog (exceptions: Pink Floyd, Iron Butterfly). The giants of prog are Genesis (early), Yes, and Emerson, Lake and Palmer. Rush are also prog, but they're from Canada and were late starters. Many more answered prog's call, but few were up to the task.

> **Suppose I was an orphan and I was sick.**
> **I'd like to think that I would get free medical care.**
>
> **At whose expense?**
>
> **At the state's expense.**
>
> **The state? Well where does the state get this**
> **marvelous magic money?**
>
> **Tax.**
>
> **Exactly. Well, maybe I don't wanna pay tax.**
> **There's the Salvation Army and all those voluntary**
> **organizations. Don't you think all those could look after**
> **those welfare systems where they are necessary?**
>
> Argument between an *NME* journalist and Rush drummer/political
> philosopher Neil Peart in 1978

LONGEST PROG SONGS

Jethro Tull – "Thick as a Brick" (43:50)

Emerson, Lake and Palmer (ELP) – "Karn Evil 9" (29:23)

Genesis – "Supper's Ready" (22:54)

Yes – "Gates of Delirium" (21:53)

Yes – "Ritual" (21:35)

ELP – "Tarkus" (20:38)

Yes – "The Remembering" (20:38)

Rush – "2112" (20:33)

Yes – "The Revealing Science of God" (20:27)

Rush – "The Fountain of Lamneth" (19:57)

Yes – "The Ancient" (18:34)

Yes – "Close to the Edge" (18:12)

Rush – "Cygnus X-1" (18:08)

Yes – "Awaken" (15:38)

Rush – "Xanadu" (11:07)

THE REVEALING SCIENCE OF GOD ETC.

There are two schools of thought in amateur musicologist circles as to the lyrics in prog. One school pores over them endlessly, interpreting the imagery, marveling at their breathtaking poetic scope, and laying bare the profound themes at the heart of the work. The other thinks they're all a load of pretentious rubbish. Rush, the Johnny-come-latelies of the prog scene (their first real prog album was 1975's *Caress of Steel*), were capable of decently indecipherable epics, usually based on some book they'd read. They got themselves into a bit of hot water, for example, when they based their 1976 album *2112* on the writings of Ayn Rand, a Russian émigré who was fiercely anti-communist, pro-capitalist, and, some say, a bit too right-wing for comfort. Jon Anderson of Yes contented himself with loosely basing the band's epic "Gates of Delirium" (which took up an entire side of the album *Relayer*—another prog giveaway) on Leo Tolstoy's *War and Peace*.

> It's not really a concept album. It's probably closer to the lyrical content of [the Who's] *Tommy*, rather than [Yes's] *Tales from Topographic Oceans.*
> Genesis keyboard player Tony Banks on their concept album *The Lamb Lies Down on Broadway*

ARTISTIC LICENSE

Without Roger Dean's artwork and stage sets (for Yes), the world of prog wouldn't have been so lush, so mysterious, so mythical and even proto-ecological. Born in 1944, Roger Dean studied at the Canterbury School of Art and the Royal College of Art Furniture school, graduating in 1968. He designed the seating in Ronnie Scott's Jazz Club, and then Ronnie commissioned him to design the album cover for a band he was managing called Gun, a London-based trio, two of whom were sons of the Kinks' road manager, Sam Curtis.

Roger then found himself designing a series of jazz album covers: "Very austere exercises, with no chance of showing off the paintings at all," says Roger now. It wasn't until he designed the cover for the first Osibisa (the African/Caribbean septet responsible for the excellent hit "Sunshine Day") album in 1971, replete with flying insect elephants, that he developed the style we all now recognize as the quintessential 1970s prog fantasy imagery.

Later in 1971, he designed the cover for the Yes album *Fragile*. Crucially, this also involved him designing the band's new logo. When he designed the triple (yes, triple) live album *Yessongs*, the gatefold was so complex that he patented it. Roger Dean's instantly recognizable style made a brief revival in contemporary music when he was employed by power-pop genius Matthew Sweet for the lettering on his 1997 album *Blue Sky on Mars*.

OTHER BANDS OF PROG STRIPE

Henry Cow
Canterbury scene, more jazzy and experimental than prog really, not vast enough.

Caravan
Another Canterbury band; not truly prog—too restrained.

Soft Machine
Yet another Canterbury band, this one with Robert Wyatt on drums and singing. Not bloated and self-important enough to really count as prog.

Camel
Yet more Canterbury, had prog desires, but always remained too quiet for full proggery.

Greenslade
The Roger Dean covers gave them the prog look; two keyboard players, one of whom was Dave Greenslade, gave them stacks and stacks of prog points.

Van der Graaf Generator
Genesis labelmates who had saxophones. Only one of their albums charted, making it to number 47. Too left-field to be proper prog. Influential beyond their commercial success with some post-punk bands.

Gentle Giant
Cover notes from their second album, *Acquiring the Taste*: "It has taken every shred of our combined musical and technical knowledge . . . to expand the frontiers of contemporary popular music." Throw in references to Rabelais, and bingo: one unsuccessful prog masterpiece!

Jade Warrior
Tull-ish thanks to the flute; released three albums but never really got anywhere.

Focus
Hammond organ/flute-driven Dutch yodeling prog four-piece. Had a big hit single with "Hocus Pocus."

The Enid
The pastoral, epic, symphonic life's work from great British eccentric Robert John Godfrey, often seen wearing an immense bushy beard, and brown corduroy trousers, standing behind his keyboards waving his fists in ecstasies of prog patriotism—due for a major rediscovery.

LOOK AT ALL OUR EXPENSIVE GEAR, YOU PEASANTS

The more equipment, the more prog the band. Check out the booklet on the 1971 Yes album *Fragile*. Each band member gets his own page. This is another dead giveaway. Prog egos are vast; these are not mere *bands*, you understand, these are virtuosi, and you shall worship them—and their guitars. Steve Howe poses with no less than 17 different stringed instruments on his page.

This is telling the earnest prog fanboy (it was/still is nearly always boys) in his suburban bedroom the following: (1) Steve Howe can play them all and that makes him a *god*. (2) He is wealthy enough to spend loads of cash on a load of really smart electric guitars, including several vintage Gretsch Country Gentleman guitars, *and* a load of expensive, hand-built acoustic guitars, *and* a load of mandolins, which are just for the three-second mandolin solo in the middle of *Tales from Topographic Oceans*, and that

makes him a *god*. (3) He is so much better and cleverer at everything than you are, therefore you shall worship him as a *god*.

Pink Floyd laid out all their equipment on the cover of their 1968 album *Ummagumma*, but this doesn't count because it pre-dates the official Start of Prog (March 19, 1971, the release date of *The Yes Album*), and because Pink Floyd never were, nor did they ever become, a prog group. Emerson, Lake and Palmer, on the other hand, were a very competitive prog group, and they had three vast trucks to carry their equipment around. One truck had an enormous E painted on the top, another had L, and the third, well, need we go on? It made a very impressive sight for passing aircraft, and birds. Keith Emerson's collection of complex, room-sized synthesizers often towered over him on stage, prompting John Peel to conclude the band was "a waste of electricity."

> **It's not a dressing gown. It cost me £60 and I had it made in Carnaby Street. It stinks something awful, but it's part of me.**
> Ian Anderson of Jethro Tull about his trampy old coat/dressing gown thing

RICK WAKEMAN V. YES

By 1973, Yes had achieved such massive popularity with their ponderous musical outpourings that they felt they were able to release a double album (80 minutes) containing just four side-long tracks. *Tales from Topographic Oceans* was a concept album based on the footnote on page 83 of an obscure religious text Jon Anderson had read while the band were on tour in Japan.

The album was 80 minutes of oblique twaddle that keyboard player Rick Wakeman described as being a "padded bra" of an album (all show and no content). To add to the sheer prog arrogance of the whole affair, Yes chose to play this album live, in its entirety, before it had been released. Even hardened Yes fans found this hard to stomach. During one performance, Rick Wakeman was so bored that he sent his roadie out to fetch him a curry, and he ate it on stage, balancing the aluminium containers on his many keyboards. Rick left the band soon after.

Lest you go away thinking that his down-to-earth role in the *Topographic Oceans* saga makes Rick Wakeman a rare voice of sanity in the world of prog gone mad, think again. The caped ivory tinkler was fully capable of producing concept albums of his own that were every bit as preposterous and overblown as the guff Yes had been coming out with. *The Six Wives of Henry VIII*, for example, came out early in 1973 and was followed by 1974's *Journey to the Centre of the Earth*, which featured the London Symphony Orchestra, whom he then took on tour around the world (bankrupting himself in the process).

His next solo album, *Myths and Legends of King Arthur and the Knights of the Round Table*, was performed live—*on ice*. It was Wakeman, it should be remembered, whose solo contribution to the 1971 Yes album *Fragile* was a classical music pastiche called "Cans and Brahms." He also had a heart attack when he was in his mid-20s, which isn't particularly prog, but is interesting nevertheless.

gods of rock

ESSENTIAL PROG LISTENING

ELP – *Tarkus* (1971)
With its weird tank/armadillo cartoon cover, *Tarkus* is a stark exercise
in flashy prog danger with a concept about said tank/armadillo thing battling
it out with a/the Manticore, whatever that is.

ELP – *Brain Salad Surgery* (1973)
A scary H. R. Giger cover, prog versions of William Blake's "Jerusalem" and
Argentinian composer Alberto Ginastera's Toccata, plus the side-long-plus-a-
bit-more "Karn Evil 9" make this a prog classic/horror, depending
on your perspective on these things.

Genesis – *Foxtrot* (1972)
Issued just a month after *Close to the Edge*, Genesis pump some prog beef
and record the side-long piece "Supper's Ready."

Genesis – *The Lamb Lies Down on Broadway* (1974)
Gabriel bailed from Genesis after this album, Genesis's most realized
and oblique concept. Some great heavy moments, particularly on
the sinister "Back in NYC."

Yes – *Fragile* (1972)
Here, with Rick Wakeman freshly on board, Yes are merely starting
to flex their prog muscles with Yes classics like "Roundabout" and
"Heart of the Sunrise."

Yes – *Close to the Edge* (1972)
Within the year (they cranked 'em out in those days), Yes managed their first
"album as concept" piece. Drummer Bill Bruford wisely quit the band after
this album, saying he'd gone as far he could with them.

YES V. ELP

Who was the most prog? It's a question that divides prog lovers along sectarian lines. On the one hand, there's ELP, a three-piece of techno-flash, cover versions of Aaron Copland tunes played at blistering pace, Hammond organ abuse, and solos. Their egos appeared to know no limits. From their debut album, ELP were unabashed about showing their faces on their record covers like crazed dictators. Despite being no lookers, their third album's cover was an oil painting (well, okay, a crappy airbrush painting) of the trio, looking off into the mid-distance, apparently topless, a light breeze blowing through their flowing locks. It's all slightly homo-erotic, the kind of image the Romans would have put on their album covers if they'd had them (and if they had, they would definitely have been bang into prog). ELP soon went even more crazy with 1973's *Brain Salad Surgery*, with a fancy die-cut cover designed by H. R. Giger (who later designed the creature and its horrific environment in *Alien*), plus a poster with three huge soft-focus pics of E, L, and, yes, P. Their 1974 triple album, *Welcome Back My Friends* . . . is an exercise in excess that was only surpassed by their unbearably vain offering *Works Volume* in 1977, by which point the prog Goliath had been all but slain by the punk David.

MOST EXPENSIVE PROG STUFF

Yes – Japanese box set of five CDs (reissues of *Fragile*, *Close to the Edge*, *Yessongs*, *Topographic Oceans*, and *Relayer*. You had to pre-order this from a record shop in Japan to get hold of a copy): **$625-plus**

Genesis – "The Knife"; seven-inch single (very rare, picture sleeve, in mint condition, naturally): **$625-plus**

Genesis – Japanese CD reissue set (reissues of all albums from *Trespass* to *Calling All Stations*): **$625-plus**

Yes – *Tales from Topographic Oceans* reel-to-reel: **$265**

Rush – *Permanent Waves* album (first issue with slightly different artwork; they airbrushed out a newspaper headline on subsequent pressings): **$175**

ELP – Japanese CD version of *Works*: **$265-plus**

ELP – *The Return of the Manticore* four-CD box set: **$90**

> **There is always a danger with any band where the musicianship is so good, that you do things that are basically showing off and lose track of the people that are going to hear an album and get satisfaction from [it].**
> Jon Anderson of Yes in a rare moment of prescience

ARE RADIOHEAD AND MUSE NEO-PROG?

Not really. Lengthy songs, a decent education, and intellectual intensity alone doth not a prog band make. Muse's expensive spaceship videos do expose what could be called prog-esque tendency for squandering large sums of money on essentially vacuous, overblown statements that serve only to make the band appear as *gods*, dude. But there is more than a hint of self-aware humor in their work, and while Jethro Tull was capable of tipping a wink in that direction, the post-modernism of pop music in the 21st century doesn't really allow for unabashed progging out. And Radiohead are just too plain clever to be a neo-prog outfit. No, neo-prog are bands who actually want to be Genesis (early), Yes, or ELP. Marillion was neo-prog, as were Pendragon and Pallas. Real neo-prog has the distinction of being almost entirely awful with no redeeming features whatsoever. A band who cite their main influence as Marillion (Poland's Abraxas, for example) are unlikely to excite the casual explorer.

WHAT ABOUT KING CRIMSON?

Brainy dudes, long songs, poly-rhythms, an ex-member of Yes (drummer Bill Bruford): It all *looks* prog, but somehow Crimson (for that is how they are referred to by the cognoscenti) are not prog, despite many efforts to categorize them as such. There has always been an icy experimentalism about Robert Fripp's work that has placed him beyond the fairy world of prog, and the big-booted, flashy-cape-wearing side of things. His association with David Bowie (the guitars on *Heroes et al.*) and the band's 1980 reinvention with Adrian Belew has conspired to give King Crimson's work a new-wave feel, and that is not something prog can boast. Real prog always has the faint aroma of decaying dinosaur flesh about it.

MOST PROG COSTUMES

Ian Anderson
Famous for his stinking dressing gown thing, which made him look like a tramp from 19th-century England. Also adorned himself with multicolored silk scarves.

Jon Anderson
During his spiritual phase, the high-voiced Yes front man took to wearing all-white stage outfits, which made him glow on stage.

Keith Emerson
Often wore a padded spaceman outfit, making him look like an extra from *Dr. Who*.

Peter Gabriel
Became infamous for his on-stage theatricality and the large number of costume changes he made during gigs, his most famous being the large flower he wore around his face. Gabriel also shaved an extra-wide part into his head (about three inches), prompting questions about his mental balance.

Rick Wakeman
Sported a wide selection of spangly capes, which gave everyone the impression that he was a kind of keyboard magician. Which, in many ways, he was.

PROG'S LOWER DIVISIONS

Languishing in the shadows of the mighty Yes, ELP, and Genesis (early) were the little leaguers: bands with big ideas, side-long concepts based on obscure novels (or the Bible), long hair, and virtuoso players. But they never quite made the step into the arenas. All are now respected, and their back catalogs collectible. There was Gentle Giant, produced by Martin Rushent, who later made his name as the in-house producer for the synth scene of the 1980s thanks to his work on the Human League's *Dare*. Another was Greek duo Aphrodite's Child, whose album *666: Apocalypse of St. John* was Demis Roussos and Vangelis on a biblical prog trip. Then there was Khan, who released only the one album, in 1972, and featured Steve Hillage. Perhaps the ultimate prog concept album to have been entirely forgotten comes from Swede Bo Hansson: *Lord of the Rings*. He did another "inspired by" album a few years later, this time based on the bunny novel *Watership Down*.

gods of rock

LET'S NOT FORGET THE TULL

Jethro Tull's success in America was solid enough that they were able to tour here in 1970, taking Yes along as their support. They were eclipsed by Yes in the end, but Tull carved out a special place in the affections of the early-1970s long-haired crowd. Jethro Tull's bearded, tramplike front man, Ian Anderson, was famous for playing flute solos while standing on one leg, like some kind of prog flamingo. Tull had been around since 1968, playing a bluesy, jazzy hard rock that won them a spot in the Rolling Stones Beatles-wannabe movie, *Rock 'n' Roll Circus*. Their second album, 1969's *Stand Up*, featured the single "Living in the Past." It reached number 3 in the charts, and the album did even better. It had an "interpretation" of Bach's Bourrée, a very prog thing to do. By 1971's album *Aqualung*, their popularity had led to confusion among the public as to the identity of the singer: Was he, in fact, Jethro Tull himself? Or was he the mysterious Aqualung? No, he was Ian Anderson. A bit like Debbie Harry's name isn't Blondie, and there is no one called Pink Floyd. Tull's ultimate prog statement was the 1972 album *Thick as a Brick*, one piece of music spanning both sides of the disc.

GENESIS – A TALE OF TWO BANDS

Genesis was once a band that formed at Charterhouse public school in 1967 and didn't have a hairy yob called Phil Collins playing drums (he joined in 1970). By 1971's *Nursery Cryme*, their third album, Peter Gabriel's Genesis was a fully fledged prog outfit. Genesis brought a pastoral, whimsical edge to prog, laced with nightmarish Victorian gothica, thanks to Gabriel's cultured lyrics. Not for him the celestial psychobabble of Yes's Jon Anderson, nor the peculiarly macho brutishness of ELP. Genesis albums were full of stories of suicidal restaurant owners called Harold the Barrel, or Victorian explorers discovering plants that then go on murderous rampages. By 1972, Genesis, too, had succumbed to the side-long epic. "Supper's Ready," from the *Foxtrot* album, remains a prog must-have. Another is the double concept album *The Lamb Lies Down on Broadway* (1974). Gabriel left in 1975 to pursue a solo career and Genesis continued, gradually succumbing to Collins's more mainstream aspirations.

The geek shall inherit the earth

THE ANTIDOTE TO THE ROCK MONSTER

WHY GEEKS?

Because there's always been a solid geek presence in rock 'n' roll, and they've always provided a much-needed counterbalance to the jock mentality that rock 'n' roll so often celebrates. Without geeks, all our pop music would have been the work of bozo school-president types like Dave Lee Roth and other macho idiots with planet-sized egos. They would happily have turned rock 'n' roll into one big playground where they were the bullies, showing off to impress girls, bench-pressing 200-pound weights, admiring each other's grotesque physiques, and turning nerds upside down for their lunch money while simultaneously playing interminable and artless guitar solos. So the geek rock star provides the millions of oppressed teenagers out there with a much-needed role model: Study hard, wear those braces, get into difficult angular music, and you, too, can get up on that stage and pull chicks. Oh, I mean, express your artistic vision in a nonsexist and appealingly gawky way that some chicks like.

JACK BLACK

If you sliced the movie star/wannabe rock star Jack Black in half, he would have the word *geek* written there, like a piece of Brighton rock. Evidence? His adoration of early 1970s rock is fully explored in minute detail in the film *School of Rock* (which is a kind of *Revenge of the Nerds* genre piece in itself). He plays (as he often does) a lovable loser in the film (which had Jim O'Rourke, an immense rock geek and guitarist for Sonic Youth, as its musical consultant). Consider also his role in *High Fidelity*, a film written by a music nerd (Nick Hornby) about geeky boys who run a record shop but have no life outside of their ability to name obscure 1980s underground bands and look down with disdain on customers who ask for records by mainstream bands. Add to the mix Black's own comedy rock outfit, Tenacious D, whose humor depends on the listener's familiarity with the various rock tropes they are parodying, and you have one big rock geek right there.

GREAT GEEK ALBUMS

Aphex Twin – *Selected Ambient Works* (1994)
Perhaps more geeky would be Aphex Twin devotee Mike Paradinas
and his µ-zik project, but this Aphex Twin album really hits the spot
for geek-boy electronica.

Devo – *Q: Are We Not Men? A: We Are Devo!* (1978)
All self-respecting music collections should include this album.
It's a jittery, anxious post-punk, pre-new-wave masterpiece that
includes the band's theme tune, "Jock Homo," and their hilariously
robotic cover version of the Rolling Stones' "Satisfaction."

Pulp – *Different Class* (1995)
The album with "Common People" on it, and probably Jarvis Cocker's
most successfully realized moment. The previous album, *His 'n' Hers*,
is great, too.

Silver Sun – *Silver Sun* (1997)
An album so stuffed with power-pop exuberance, shrill melodies, and
lovely harmonies that it's a crime against pop that the singles lifted
from it didn't become huge hits.

Talking Heads – *Fear of Music* (1979)
Some may try to convince you otherwise, but this, their third, is
Talking Heads' best album. Produced by Brian Eno, there are no hits
on it (they came with the next couple of albums), but it encompasses
Byrne's poetic otherness perfectly.

> **I think music can achieve more reality than
> any other art form at the moment. It has
> more depth: you're dealing with as direct a
> brain-to-brain communication as possible.**
> David Thomas, Pere Ubu

gods of rock

GEEK CHIC

Anorak
Quilted — for the hard-core "no friends" nerd only.

Badges
Featuring obscure and mostly wet indie bands, generally handmade or vintage items, purchased at great expense off eBay.

Briefcase
With buckles — for holding fanzines, Sarah Records seven-inch singles, and books of poetry.

Clark's shoes
The school type, not the ones favored by mods.

Gloverall duffel coat
Like Paddington Bear; probably the most economically significant investment in clothing a geek can make.

Horn-rimmed specs
Specs that are in fact very expensive but look like they might have been issued by the Boy Scouts between 1962 and 1974.

V-neck sweater
Private-school gray for punk geek.

BUDDY HOLLY

Buddy Holly, the bootlace-tie-wearing rock 'n' roller who had an unwavering ear for a pop tune, is the Godfather of Geek. He wore glasses, had a slightly awkward demeanor, and was certainly no Elvis Presley in the looks department. But his ability to write hook-laden pop tunes, one after the other, gave him international fame. In 1958, he toured the UK, where the yet-to-be-famous John Lennon and Paul McCartney saw him (March 20, at Liverpool's Empire Theatre) and were inspired. They even named their band the Beatles (in case you'd forgotten) as a tribute to Holly's Crickets. Tragically, an airplane crash ended Buddy Holly's career early, but he left behind a canon of songs that is acknowledged as among the most important and influential in the history of rock 'n' roll.

GEEKS: KNOW THINE ENEMY — JOCK ROCKERS

Dave Lee Roth
1980s spandex clown
Jet
Greasy rockers from Down Under — avoid
Liam Gallagher
Leary lug, soccer fan

TALKING HEADS

David Byrne arrived in the world's consciousness as the twitchy guy singing about being a psycho killer, fronting Talking Heads, New York's latest export from CBGB, the gloomy run-down bar on the Bowery. Skinny, bespectacled, and with a strange whiny voice, Byrne was an unlikely pop star. He was too straight to be punk, not quite as studiously cool as New York contemporaries Television—and they weren't about guitar solos, which Television were. Yet his band would turn out to be one of the most popular to vault out of the post-punk scene to enjoy international success. They baffled a great many people when they started having big hit singles, and Byrne became famous for a while (thanks to the concert film *Stop Making Sense*) for his preposterously large white suit. When asked why he wore such a suit, Byrne's deadpan response was: "Because it makes my head look small."

Talking Heads finally broke up in 1996, and Byrne is now a much-respected figure making music for grown-ups; he has developed strong interests in music from around the world that's not rooted in rock 'n' roll. His 1997 solo album *Feelings* features guest appearances from Devo's Mark Mothersbaugh and Jerry Casale, squaring that particular geek circle nicely.

Thanks! Does anyone have any questions?
David Byrne in concert with Talking Heads

gods of rock

BRIT GEEK DOES EXIST

The last three decades has seen the emergence of major music geeks in the UK. The geek of the 1970s was Gary Numan, his emotionless persona clearly developed through a childhood of solitude for "being weird." In the 1980s, Thomas Dolby burst into the charts with his frenetic nerd anthem "She Blinded Me with Science." He looked like a mad professor and played up to it. But then it turned out he was an actual techno-geek in the Bill Gates mold when he started his own technology company Beatnik Inc., which created ringtones for cell phones, and started appearing as a guest speaker at major technology conferences. In the 1990s, when it seemed that the dispiriting culture of macho was victorious (Blur and Oasis slugging it out for tabloid headlines and droning on about soccer), it was Pulp's Jarvis Cocker who was flying the flag for the Brit geek constituency. He was physically awkward, intelligent, trained in art, and had been trying to get his band known for nearly 15 years when they finally broke through as the unlikeliest of the Britpop bands. He continued to sing about the underdog loser, a position he was intimately familiar with, and established himself as the UK's best-loved eccentric of the age.

ELVIS COSTELLO: FAKE GEEK?

The first great controversy to hit Elvis Costello's career was when it was noticed that Elvis didn't have proper lenses in his glasses. Did this mean that his whole geek-chic shtick—the specs, the haircut, the clothes, the peculiar stance (with his knees locked together, his feet wide apart)—was *fake*? Had he merely adopted that Buddy Holly look as some kind of cynical marketing ploy, much the same as the equally fake name he went under? (His real name is Declan Patrick MacManus; he swiped the Elvis from Presley, and Costello was his mother's maiden name.) But does any of this detract from the explosive quality of his first recordings? Well, no. But dishing out a widely reported racist insult about Ray Charles during an argument with American singer Bonnie Bramlett, *that* might have. Recording a country-and-western album (1981's *Almost Blue*) and then putting a sticker on it that read WARNING. THIS STICKER CONTAINS COUNTRY AND WESTERN MUSIC AND MAY CAUSE OFFENSE TO NARROW-MINDED LISTENERS didn't help, either.

GEEKISH BANDS/PERFORMERS

Depeche Mode
Now they are continent-conquering synth rock monster
cross-dressing leather drug-survivor stars, but when they emerged,
blinking into the limelight from their native Essex back in 1980,
they were a bunch of nerdy schoolboys with acne.

Devo
Donning yellow chemical-protection suits, matching plastic hairdos, and
"flowerpot" hats, the De-Evolution Band were perhaps the ultimate geeks.

Gary Numan
Now a hard-rocking guitar guy, Numan was at his best as an alienated boy
with bad skin playing arid synth tunes and singing about feeling safe in his
car in his nasal whine. Used his cash to fund his hobby of flying airplanes.

Pere Ubu
Another band, like Devo, from the industrial wastelands around
Cleveland/Akron, Ohio. Singer David Thomas was (is) a portly gentleman
who often performed wearing a suit. Brainy lyrics.

Silver Sun
Fantastic Britpop power outfit built around the talents of James Broad, a
bespectacled Buddy Holly look-alike with a penchant for Rush. Big in Japan.

Wheatus
Formed in 1988 by Brendan B. Brown, they had a huge hit with "Teenage
Dirtbag" and then lost their major record deal because Brendan insisted on
producing the follow-up album. The band next re-released an album on their
own label called *Suck Fony*, a spoonerism aimed at ex-paymasters, Sony.

> **I was so into *Star Wars*—my favorite figure was
> Hammerhead, the band player in the bar—that
> when my sister was born, in 1977, I persuaded
> my parents to name her Leia.**
> Brian Bell, Weezer

WEEZER

"I grew up in various little farm towns in upstate Connecticut sheltered from anything remotely 'cool,'" says Weezer main man Rivers Cuomo. He was brought up by hippie parents (hence his name—he has a brother called Leaves) on a Hindu ashram, something that didn't exactly help the young Cuomo blend into mainstream American life. He also had one leg longer the other and wore glasses. He moved to LA to "become a rock star" with his band Avant Garde, but all that happened was that his girlfriend left him, his band broke up, and he was left feeling "really sad," so he started writing songs to express his emotions, as he was incapable of talking about "anything real." All this geek misery turned around when Cuomo formed his new band, Weezer, in 1992 and signed with Geffen in 1994. The song "Buddy Holly," with double nostalgia promo video based on the 1970s show *Happy Days* (itself a geek-fest), was bundled with the Windows 95 computer operating software system (how geeky is *that*?), and gave Weezer a huge hit, the cash from which enabled Cuomo to have corrective surgery to his leg. Ten years later, Weezer are still having hits, and Cuomo is one hefty geek success story.

OTHER SPECCIE GEEKS

Kurt Cobain – Donned specs for a while to relate to the high-school underdog. Famously despised his increasingly jock following.
Graham Coxon – Often drunk ex-Blur guitarist with very geeky solo career on the go.
Franz Ferdinand – No specs here, but utterly rooted in geek legend worship. May well wear specs in private.
John Lennon – Ultimate spec-wearing rocker, made granny specs cool but used to avoid wearing his early-1960s horn-rimmed glasses, although they were way cool, too.
Lisa Loeb – A rare lady geek.
Manfred Mann – College geek-out, much-heavy specs and bowl haircuts. Good pop. Except for "Blinded by the Light."
The Muffs – Anti-jock, girl-fronted power-pop trio. With specs.
Andy Partridge – Front man of the hugely geeky XTC. They released the very excellent album *English Settlement*.
Sloan – Canadian power pop, Halifax geek.

I can't stop rockin',
no, I can't stop rockin'.
Well, I can't stop rockin',
baby, till I lose my mind.

ZZ Top

FURTHER READING

Bass Culture, Lloyd Bradley
Celluloid Jukebox, edited by Jonathan Romney and Adrian Wootton
Dear Boy: The Life of Keith Moon, Tony Fletcher
Digital Gothic: A Critical Discography of Tangerine Dream, Paul Stump
Hammer of the Gods, Stephen Davis
Hungry for Heaven, Steve Turner
I'm with the Band, Pamela Des Barres
Keyfax 2, Julian Colbeck
Kraftwerk: Man, Machine and Music, Pascal Bussy
Like a Rolling Stone: Bob Dylan at the Crossroads, Greil Marcus
Melody Maker Classic Rock Interviews, edited by Allan Jones
Openers II, Roky Erikson
Psychotic Reactions and Carburetor Dung, Lester Bangs
Q: Are We Not Men? A: We Are Devo!, Jade Dellinger and David Giffels
Rock and Roll: The Movies, Rob Burt
Rock 'n' Roll Babylon, Gary Herman
The Beatles Diary, Barry Miles
The Beatles: Off the Record, Keith Badman
The Guinness Book of Hit Singles 2004
The Guinness Who's Who of Heavy Metal, edited by Colin Larkin
The Guinness Who's Who of Indie and New Wave, edited by Colin Larkin
The Guinness Who's Who of Reggae, edited by Colin Larkin
The Lives of John Lennon, Albert Goldman
The Ultimate Beatles Encyclopedia, Bill Harry
Waiting for the Man, Harry Shapiro

INDEX

INDEX